CHICAGO: *THE SECOND CITY*

CHICAGO:

THE SECOND CITY

BY *A. J.* _{bbott oseph} *LIEBLING*

DRAWINGS BY STEINBERG

1
9
5
2

NEW YORK: ALFRED A. KNOPF

To **R. R. McC.**

Foreword

■■

The day after the first of my series of three pieces on Chicago appeared in *The New Yorker* I began getting letters from Chicagoans and people who had merely been there. The letters from the visitors, and from expatriates, were almost all favorable—those from people who were still there weren't. The most catamountainous of all came from the suburbs; the people who wouldn't live in the city if you gave them the place rose to its defense like fighters off peripheral airfields in the Ruhr in 1944.

There was for example the woman from Oak Park, Illinois, who wrote:

If my old sainted grandmother, in her eighties, who having borne eleven children, reared them successfully to maturity, now spends her life in prayer and uncomplaining illness, had been brought upon a dias [*sic*] and examined dispassionately by a jury of casting directors I could not have been more dismayed or indignant.

All the letter-writers together found just two, or perhaps three, small factual errors, which I have signalized in the present book by footnotes in the appropriate places. The most considerable was that I had placed the Bahai temple in Evanston, the suburb just north of Chicago, when it was really in Wilmette, a mile farther on. But most of the objections were directed against the spirit of the reporting, which the objectors found too objective: *De mortuis nihil nisi bonum,* and "Don't cheer, men, the poor devils are dying," were the two main lines of rebuke. Both are too pessimistic, for Chicago is neither dead nor dying; it is, as the sideshow men say, "Alive, Alive—did you ever see a two-headed baby?"

("The gaff in that line," a sideshow man once told me— he happened to be a Chicagoan—"is that you don't say you got a live two-headed baby. You just ask them have they seen one." But this is a digression.)

Another kind of unobserved fire, thrown in my general direction, was the charge that I was a flitting viewer, writing about the place after a visit of a few weeks, days, or hours (according to the degree of indignation of the writer). The extreme example of this form of criticism I have preserved in a postcard from a lady named Swift. It bears the simple legend: "You were never in Chicago."[1]

But the fact is that I lived in Chicago for nearly a year in 1949–50 and went back to check up in May, 1951. So this isn't a between-trains job. I gathered a lot of material which I discarded; the report is packed down rather than built up, and I think it is exact, in the same sense as El Greco's picture of Toledo, not the one in Ohio. The suppressed detail would, if retained, merely have messed things up. I don't say it is as good as the El Greco, but Saul Steinberg has tried to bridge the gap with his illustrations.

The least easily answerable comment came via postcard from a man in Bergenfield, New Jersey, who had read the first section to appear in *The New Yorker*.

"Re Chicago:" the message read, "Okay, we give up, . . . who asked you?"

To which I can but rejoin, "Who asked Lemuel Gulliver or Marco Polo or Tocqueville or Sir John Mandeville or Abyssinian Bruce? Who asked Dam Trollope or Son Trollope, Birkbeck (who got to Illinois in 1817) or Mungo Park

....

[1] I replied with a quotation from "Take Back Your Mink": "It all seems a HORRIBLE DREAM."

ix

or William Dampier? In fact, what travel writer ever
waited to be asked?"

Lest these precedents be thought insufficient, I invoke that
of Colonel Robert Rutherford McCormick. Annually, or
almost, the Colonel quits his atomic-bombproof eyrie in his
Symphony in Stone, the Tribune Tower, to soar off into
the Wild Blue Yonder on a mission of aerial reportage.
From the places where he alights, the Colonel tells *Tribune*
readers what the world outside looks like to him, generally
pretty awful. The average time it takes him to cover a country is twenty-four hours. And if the Colonel can tell Chicago
about the outside world, why can't a fellow from the latter tell
the outside world about Chicago? To borrow a line from
Judy Holliday, it's a free country.

Some of the letters I got, even from Chicago, took a more
sympathetic turn. As one of these put it:

> It is, and most apparently so, that Chicago is not
> what it should or could be. It is not, however, in need
> of more bitter criticicizing, rather in need of intelli-
> gent and honest aid at the front.
>
> I should like to know Mr. Lieblings true humanitarian
> capacity—if any!! It is hardly likely that he throws
> automobile tires at his wife, beats same, plus children,—
> nor would he, upon encountering a person of lowest
> circumstances,—"a beggar on the street" (New York
> version)—"a bum" (Chicago version, and quite the
> more vivid and descriptive term)—probably be cap-

tured with the near obsesion of just how he could further
lead this be-beggared one into still further depths of
any worse condition which might be possible to bring
about.—It is entirely enough that there are now, so
many others, world wide, who are only too willing to
trample any of the falling, hesitant, or be-clouded—
without dwelling so long, hard and sarcasticly upon
such an accumulance of dowdy and brutal remarks,
which in the end, are certainly not much of a shock
to anyone,—

Is Mr. Liebling forming a "Be Nasty to Chicago
Club"??? Is he perhaps trying to gain followers—
those who are also inclined towards sarcasium, slicing
throats,— Or is he by some maddening theme—perhaps
without knowing, himself endeavoring to inspire helpful
people to action at the Chicago front!! If this is so
and I almost entirely doubt such a pleasant ulterior
motive, then I should adore to board the next plane
possible and be first in line to tenderly and encouragingly grasp the hand of Mr. Liebling as he staggers
(I hope) backward from reading such reactionaries
as this one of many of which he must be in recipience
daily!

Leave us not without exception, stamp on the discarded cigarette—if it is out, it's quite ridiculous.—

Sincerely,

A first emotional letter to the editors writer.

First-Emotional-Letter-To-The-Editors-Writer has divined, although with pardonable incredulity, the true intent of this report, which is kind. I stagger forward (I hope) to tenderly and encouragingly grasp his or her hand. His or her reactionary is most perceptive.

Even kinder was a man who might have claimed a just grievance, since he had to carry pounds of my prose on his daily rounds, as well as pay for his own copy.

"Mr. Liebling," he wrote, from an address far out on the North Side:

> By this time no doubt you'll have batches of mail excoriating you for your series on Chicago. Well, here's one reader (subscriber) who finds little sniffishness in your pieces. . . .
>
> I'm not a literary person; I don't know any writers or hang around book stores. I'm a mailman (we dislike *postman*—for the same reason editors sneer at *journalist*). Born here in '96, a few blocks from where the Chicago fire started in '71, I have lived here practically all my life, with the exception of about five years in New York and the East. So I can honestly cast my vote for your excellent reporting as a native son.

I have embodied a considerable amount of the more pertinent correspondence in my footnotes to this present text, and added a few of my own reactionaries to those of which I have been in recipience.

A. J. Liebling

Contents

CHICAGO: *THE SECOND CITY*

1.

So Proud to Be

Jammy-jammy

●●

In the summertime, the Gold Coast of Chicago, that strip of opulent apartment houses and mansions along Lake Shore Drive, takes on some of the aspects of the streets leading from the Brighton Beach station of the B.-M.T. line out in coastal Brooklyn. Large numbers of bathing-suited inhabitants of the steamy interior of the city arrive by trolley at a point a couple of blocks from Lake Shore Drive, bearing beach balls, babies, lunch hampers, and fudgicles. Making their way

3

through fine streets served by private garbage collectors (public collection is worse than irregular), the beachers pass under the marquees of buildings whose tenants drink water from which the chlorine taste of ordinary Chicago tap water has been filtered. (This service costs two dollars a month per apartment and is a more satisfactory solution of the taste problem, from a Gold Coast point of view, than having the city bring palatable water from afar for everybody, which would mean higher taxes.) The beachers do not come in automobiles, although a substantial proportion unundoubtedly possess them. ("No Money Down, No Credit Standing Necessary. Even If You Have Been Blacklisted, See Me," Chicago second-hand dealers advertise.) They would find no place near the Drive to park. The streets are bordered with "No Parking, By Order of the Police Department" signs, which are obtained from the office of a city alderman at the rate of eleven dollars a year and insure that any man who pays for one will always have a place to park his car. The beachers go through a tunnel under the Drive and emerge on a strip of concrete and sand. The sun is strong even in June, when the water is still para-

4

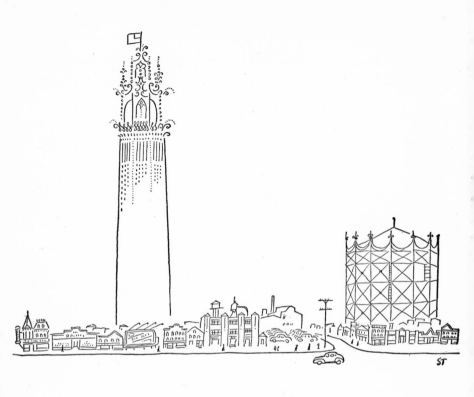

lyzingly cold. Lying on their backs, the beachers gaze out at the great empty surface of Lake Michigan, and the girls compare the discolorations of their legs. When they turn over on their bellies, they are able to look back at what skyline Chicago has to offer—a serrated wall of high buildings aligned along the lakeward side of the city. One among them is the Tribune Tower, a Gothic skyscraper equipped with a carillon of editorial tocsins.[1] So viewed, Chicago seems a big city instead of merely a large place.

But the beachers are not fooled. They know that what they see is like a theatre backdrop with a city painted on it. Immediately behind the precise middle of the palisade of tall buildings lies the Loop, a rectangle only seven blocks long and five wide, holding most of the major stores, theatres, and big hotels and office buildings, as well as the financial district, components of a city that in Manhattan are strung out from Central Park South to the Battery, a good five

....

[1] I am informed by two correspondents that the Tower, though one of the serrated wall of buildings, all right, is not visible from the Gold Coast Beach, being concealed by a curve in the shoreline. I have not been back to check.

miles, and in London from Albert Hall to the Tower, about the same. The Loop, with its lakeside screen, forms a unit like the Kremlin as described by Richard Harding Davis when he attended the coronation of Nicholas II, in 1896—a small city surrounded by a boundless agglutination of streets, dramshops, and low buildings without urban character. The Loop is like Times Square and Radio City set down in the middle of a vast Canarsie. Moreover, the façade is no more functional than a billboard turned away from the road; it might impress travellers if they approached the city from the Lake, but nobody does. The stranger arrives by car from the airport, approaching the Loop across a tundra of industrial suburbs unchanged in character by the city line, or else comes in on one of the railroads that run through slums of their own making. The railroad tracks are the cords that hold the Chicago Gulliver supine. They crisscross the town in a kind of ticktacktoe game in which the apparent object of each line is to stop its competitors from getting out of town. Thus the Baltimore & Ohio, connecting the city with the East, has

8

been obliged to head due west for five or six miles to find a chink to slip through.

This Chicago is not like the one I used to visualize in my provincial East Coast youth, but it is certainly less alarming. My first intimations of Chicago were missionary and literary, and made me feel I could do without it. When I was about eleven, a boy of around my age moved with his parents from Chicago to the town on the south shore of Long Island where I lived. He was an enthusiastic Boy Scout, and he used to tell me and other uninterested Long Island boys about the fine boulevards and parks they had in Chicago. He also said the aquarium was a lulu. The football pennants tacked to the walls of his room bore exotic names, such as Northwestern, Iowa, and Purdue, instead of names everybody knew, like Yale, Columbia, and Rutgers. That same year, my mother gave me a ten-volume set of Kipling for my birthday, and I read straight through it. The volume that contained "Wee Willie Winkie," "Baa Baa, Black Sheep," and "The Drums of the Fore and Aft" (which, I decided on reading them, were the three greatest short stories ever written) also contained "American Notes"—correspondence describing a voyage the author had made to the United States in 1889. Of Chicago, my new idol had written, "Having seen it, I urgently desire never to see it again. It is inhabited by savages. Its water is the water of the Hooghly, and its air is dirt. Also it says that it is the 'boss' town of America. I do not believe that it has anything to do with this country." Kipling caught Chicago at possibly its most terrifying moment. The census of 1890 showed that it had displaced Philadelphia as the second city of the United States, and it was preparing to go right through the roof.

It was considerably later, when I was a college senior, that I again thought of Chicago. There was some kind of literary revolution going on there. All the prose coming out of the place was highly carbonated. I read a book called "Midwest Portraits," by Harry Hansen, about this Chicago literary *Spritzer*, a book that Laurence Stallings had reviewed in the New York *World* under what I thought the side-splitting heading "Write 'Em, Cowboy." (Stallings, a native of

Georgia, was evidently under the influence of the common illusion that it is in the Far West. In reality, it is in the easternmost third of the continent.) Among the chapter headings were "Carl Sandburg, Poet of the Streets and of the Prairie," "Sherwood Anderson, Corn-fed Mystic, Historian of the Middle Age of Man," "Robert Herrick and Edgar Lee Masters, Interpreters of Our Modern World," "Harriet Monroe, Priestess of Poetry," and "Ben Hecht, Pagliacci of the Fire Escape."

Until 1938, however, I never got to see Chicago, although I had by then met the Pagliacci of the Fire Escape, who had moved to Nyack, and Hansen himself, who was doing a book column for the New York *World-Telegram*. Among the places I had seen were Angers, Funchal, Cappoquin, Youghal, Spitzbergen, and Gevrey-Chambertin, but I hadn't been west of Buffalo. By 1938, the Chicago literary revolution had ceased, except for parting bursts from the tail guns of angry young novelists flying East. The writers left behind them the question of whether what had been written about the place had ever actually existed— for example, Sandburg's city, "with lifted head singing so proud to be alive and coarse and strong and cunning." From all reports, the place was still reasonably coarse, but the pride and the singing had been muted. And instead of "laughing even as an ignorant fighter laughs who has never lost a battle," Chicago wore a grin that might have indicated punch-drunkenness.

There is an opinion, advanced by some men who worked in Chicago transiently during the twenties, as well as by many native Chicagoans, that the city did approximate the great, howling, hurrying, hog-butchering, hog-mannered challenger for the empire of the world specified in the legend, but that at some time around 1930 it stopped as suddenly as a front-running horse at the head of the stretch with a poor man's last two dollars on its nose. What stopped it is a mystery, like what happened to Angkor Vat. There are only theories, most of them too materialistic to satisfy me, such as "Sam Insull took this town for all it had" and "The depression hit this town a wallop it never shook off."[2] Some skeptics have their own ex-

---

[2] A woman with a plaintive voice, calling me on the telephone after this appeared, dated Chicago's decline from

planation of the disparity between the Chicago of the rhapsodists and the Chicago of today. It is that the rhapsodies were merely the result of mutual suggestion, like the St. Vitus's Dance epidemics of the Middle Ages. There may be some truth in that theory, too. "It was a wonderful place when I was a kid," a fellow who writes a column on foreign affairs for a Chicago paper once told me. "Guys would be shot down every day on the busiest street corners. It was roman-

the day Jane Addams boarded the Henry Ford peace ship in 1916. The intellectual life, as well as the social conscience, of Chicago, centered on Jane Addams and Hull House in the years before World War I, the woman said. Miss Addams's pacifism destroyed her prestige, consequently that of her whole group. Momentum carried some of the writers through the early twenties, and then they dispersed, having nothing to hold them together.

A couple of weeks later I had a letter from a writing friend. "Many years ago I made Chicago my home for a little more than a year," he wrote, "having left college to do social work in what was then still Jane Addams's town. And during that period I saw Chicago through the eyes of the Dell-Anderson-Masters-Sandburg-Monroe coterie. They were at the white heat of their creation in a town that was momentarily blessed with greatness. As the years have passed by my Chicago Dream has faded slowly but steadily."

The stranger on the telephone may have had something.

tic." He admitted, when I put the direct question, that he personally had not seen anybody shot, but I sensed that he did not like to acknowledge this, even to himself. (I might as well have asked a Charleston lady how she knew that everybody in the South had been rich before 1860.) Mary Garden says that in 1910 she found in Chicago a great audience and almost unlimited backing for grand opera in French. There is some tangible support for these reminiscences of the Grande Epoque—in the files of the Chicago *Tribune*, for instance, and in the existence of the now silent Civic Opera House. The *Tribune* in the twenties used to print daily on its editorial page a "Program for Chicagoland," of which Article 1 was "Make Chicago the First City of the World." Now it doesn't bother.

When I first got to Chicago, in November, 1938, I didn't even know that anything had changed. I was simply relieved to find in the city neither the newness nor the briskness that I dislike and that I had been led to expect. The Midwestern friendliness that I had been warned I would have to put up with was well dissimulated by the airport personnel. Seen from the taxi, on the long ride in from the airport, the place looked slower, shabbier, and, in defiance of all chronology, older than New York. There was an outer-London dinginess to the streets; the low buildings, the industrial plants, and the railroad crossings at grade produced less the feeling of being in a great city than of riding through an endless succession of factory-town main streets. The transition to the Loop and its tall buildings was abrupt, like entering a walled city. I found it beguilingly medieval.

I first noticed something like what I had been warned to expect when I reached, on a thoroughfare called Ashland Avenue, a point near which the city begins to look like a city. The street there is lined with bizarre stone houses that were once family residences, but of what class I have never been able to decide. They aren't mansions, but they aren't smack up against each other, either, and most of them have little spires and turrets that make them look all the more desolate now, like a bedraggled old woman in the remains of a spirited hat. The first you strike as you come from the airport have Negro tenants, who bulge out of the windows and spill down the stoops. The last are given over to far shabbier whites. On a street corner along Ashland Avenue, I noticed a large sign proclaiming, "Chicago has the finest system of boulevards and parks in the world." That sounded to me like the Boy Scout with the Purdue pennant. This form of civic self-approbation is not extinct in Chicago. A huge sign on Michigan Boulevard reads, "This is the Magnificent Mile. It is lined with the most beautiful buildings and the finest and most luxurious shops in the World." Such vestiges of the old spirit, like the *Tribune's* unchanging subtitle, "The World's Greatest Newspaper," are regarded by the inhabitants with the same kind of affection they bestow upon the old Water Tower, which survived the Fire of 1871. They are links with the plangent past. "Heiress of all the ages, she stands in the foremost files of time," the *Tribune* editorialized about Chicago in 1893.

A thing about Chicago that impressed me from the hour I got there was the saloons. New York bars operate on the principle that you want a drink or you wouldn't be there. If you're civil and don't mind waiting, they will sell you one when they get around to it.

Chicago bars assume that nobody likes liquor, and that to induce the customers to purchase even a minute quantity, they have to provide a show. Restaurateurs, I was to learn, approach the selling of food from the same angle. The Porterhouse, a restaurant in the Hotel Sherman, when I last looked in on it, had six cowboy violinists in fringed pants to play "Tales from the Vienna Woods" at your table in order to sell you a hamburger, and the menu listed credits for costume and scenic design. The urge to embellishment found literary outlet in the listing of things to eat, such as:

Ah, the PORTERHOUSE! Aristocrat of steaks . . . most delectable of steaks. Greatest of all the steaks, for within it are encompassed the Tenderloin, the Sirloin, the meaty bone of the full loin. Small wonder that in this fabulous steak, ERNEST BYFIELD found inspiration for the name of the last . . . and the finest room he was to conceive!

Carved from vintaged corn-fed beef, your PORTERHOUSE is broiled under a high heat that seals in the flavor-giving juices . . . sears the rich fat to a crispy-edged succulence. Specify to your Captain the precise degree of "doneness" you require—and tell him, too, whether you wish it to be graced with garlic's subtle savor.

One of the more modest items on the menu was "Chuck Wagon Beef Stew, Sautéd Julienne of Beef Tenderloin in Hot Sour Cream Sauce with Rice." Walking through a cocktail lounge and into another dining room in the Sherman, known as the Well of the Sea, I was handed a bill of fare proposing "Bahama Conch Chowder with Barbados Rum, said to be a favorite soup of Ernest Hemingway, believed by the natives of the Bahama Islands to promote virility and longevity" and "Scallops in Season: Called St. James Shells in England. Says Elliot Paul, 'Cleverest and most tasty of Mollusks.' " The Sherman menu writer is in the great tradition of a Chicago restaurateur named Dario Toffenetti, who opened a New York *succursale*, where, in season, he sells "Autumnal Pumpkin Pie in an Avalanche of Whipped Cream."

The smallest bars provide an organist or a pianist

or two organists or two pianists, or a pianist and an organist back to back, both backs, if female, bare to the coccyx. The musicians work on a small dais behind the bottles. Places slightly larger furnish a singer and a comedian, as well. Their art makes conversation impossible, but on my first visit to Chicago I had no one to talk to anyway, so I found it a pleasant custom. It wasn't until I went back later and made some friends in the city that I learned to long for the sociable quiet of a New York bar, in which you can snarl at your companions without having to use a microphone.[3]

The Chicago bars also employ blondes known as dice girls, who stand behind small green baize layouts and keep score on customers attempting a ten-dice game called Twenty-Six. In this game, you try to roll any number from one to six twenty-six times or better in thirteen tries, the odds against such an achievement, according to experts, being slightly less than five to one. The customary bet is a quarter, but you can play higher. If you win, the house pays four to one, which gives it a seventeen-per-cent edge. This is about the

[3] Of late, television has been cutting into the number of good snarling spots, even here.

19

same as the take of the parimutuel machines in New York State. The bar, however, pays its four to one in trade, on which there is a profit of perhaps three hundred per cent. One of my most astute Chicago friends, a native, is sure the girls can control the dice with magnets. I do not believe this for a minute, but it illustrates the working of the Chicago mind. It is inconceivable to my friend that the house should be content with the monumental advantage it already has. Yet he plays the game steadily, mostly in bars around the Loop. He loves that grim rectangle, bound in its iron crown of elevated-railroad tracks, and says that during the war, when he was overseas and he thought of Chicago, it was always of the Loop in the rain, with the sound of the low-pitched, bisyllabic police whistles, like sea birds' cries.

I began my investigation of Chicago's saloons the first evening I spent in the city, and wound up by wandering out from the center of the Loop along a street called West Madison, which resembles a Bowery of a more raucous sort than the one we know. Toward the end of my run, I found myself in an area where whiskey was two shots for a quarter—and the entertain-

ment was more copious than ever. I have never heard
"Mexicali Rose" sung so well as that night on West
Madison Street. I arrived back in my hotel filled with
that tranquil satisfaction that follows a revel in a
strange town, in which nobody will turn up next day
to remind you how dull you were.

The following afternoon, I went out to Sportsman's
Park, which was—and is—a half-mile race track,
such as one would expect to find at a county-fair meeting. Because hardly anybody will risk a good horse on
such short turns, the long spring and fall meetings
there attract a class of stables usually seen only in
places like Puerto Rico (among the winners last year
was a horse just off a successful campaign at Raton,
New Mexico), and the size of the purses and the grade
of the jockeys are scaled to the class of competition.
Only the crowds and the betting pools are city-size;
there is no other racing in Chicago while Sportsman's
is in operation. A year or so ago, the track auditor, a
man named Hugo Bennett, testified before the Kefauver Committee that he had lent eighty thousand
dollars of the track's funds to Paul (The Waiter)
Ricca, for no special reason. Ricca is reputedly a

gangster with power to influence the awarding of racing dates. Edward J. O'Hare, the first president of Sportsman's, was shot and killed on the street in 1939. The track was built originally for greyhound racing and scaled to dogs rather than horses. The gyp (for gypsy) horsemen who race there now are small owners trying to win their living in purse money and from clients who will pay for a tip. Half the horses, in my time, apparently spent race mornings with all four feet in tubs of numbing ice. Few horses are worked under saddle at Sportsman's, for fear they will break down; they are "ponied," which means that a mounted man gets out in front of them and gallops them on a lead line. To bear up under a jockey's inconsiderable weight for the duration of a race once a week is about all the trainers expect of their steeds.

Sportsman's is beyond the city line, in Cicero, a town devoted to the cult of Al Capone, who did much to put it on the map. Cicero looks no more or less sinister than any other Passaic—tarpaper roofs, frame dwellings flaking paint, and beer signs. It was in a saloon there one evening that I met a wonderful woman with a gift for capsule autobiography. She was the daughter of a Lithuanian saloonkeeper, and was flanking her father behind the bar when I stopped in. The bar was on the ground floor of their house and had surely been a home-brew or needle-beer joint before repeal came and they opened the front door. "I was once married to a rich man who manufactured printing ink," this lady told me. "But he was always too potst. So I came home to Dad."

In the barbershop at Sportsman's one morning, I saw a colored man cornered by another, whom he had pretended skillfully but unsuccessfully not to see. "How come you haven't been around since you hit that daily double?" the interceptor said. "You used to be so jammy-jammy with me." I never say potst or jammy-jammy without thinking of a city with lifted head, singing.

The second time I visited Chicago was in the early spring of 1941. My purpose in going there then was to talk with General Robert E. Wood, chairman of the board of Sears, Roebuck, and with a young man named Robert Douglas Stuart, Jr., son of a vice-president of Quaker Oats. They were chairman and national

director, respectively, of the America First Committee, an organization devoted to keeping the United
States from aiding Great Britain in her war effort.
This was also the official line of the Communist Party,
for the Soviets and the Third Reich were still jammy-
jammy, but there was no reason to suspect America First of Leninism. General Wood looked more like
a general than most generals get to look, somewhat resembling Warren Gamaliel Harding. He was also
even more positive than most generals get to be, and
told me that a German victory could not possibly en-
danger the United States, then as naked of armament
as a garden worm. The General had served in the Quar-
termaster Corps during the First World War and he
knew. He expressed no concern over what a German
victory would mean to Europe; he considered preoc-
cupation with any country other than America treason-
able. He said the Eastern seaboard didn't represent
America, whose rich, red heart, he let me understand,
beat within the walls of the Chicago Board of Trade
Building, on the eighteenth floor of which we sat talking, in the America First offices.

General Wood was obviously a decent man, but he

gave me a feeling of remoteness from the world
I knew that was even stronger than the one I had had
in Franco Spain the day I crossed the French frontier
after Pétain asked for the armistice of 1940.
The Spanish civilians at least could understand from
their own experience the meaning of conquest. The national director, nearly forty years the General's junior, was even more disquieting, because, despite his
youth, he was equally assured. All things, national
and international, were manifest to the manufacturers
of overalls and breakfast cereals, and the America
First letterhead showed that the General and the oat-
let had behind them the man who made Spam and a
man who made steel and a man who had investments
in salt, teletype machines, and wristwatches. As intellectual reference, they offered Robert Maynard
Hutchins, the president of the University of Chicago.[4]

---

[4] General Wood has a Winnetka lady fan who wrote to
me:

> Your affinity for truth reminds me of Mister Tru-
> man's affinity for integrity. Since you second-guess,
> with such moral righteousness, our General Wood (she
> must have been in the Quartermaster Corps) you evi-
> dently were and are convinced that other peoples' wel-

After we entered the war, I have been told, Chicago was gloriously hospitable to service men and at least as bellicose as any other city in the country where people were making money hand over fist. But I could not

fare is commensurate with our own. [Author's note—I had always thought that accepted Christian doctrine.] And that "America First" is either morally evil or politically impractical. An amazing conclusion from one who labels himself a "New York City first" advocate.—New York: Pinnacle of Culture . . . Phonies . . . and All The News That's Fit to Print. It never ceases to scratch your bloated pomposity, does it, that Chicago publishes the World's Greatest Newspaper? [The Chicago *Tribune.*]

Besides evoking the above thoughts, your article inspired little regard for your accuracy and perception. You grazed, sans insight, the periphery. [This apparently, refers to Winnetka's geographical position re Chicago.]

A friend of Mr. Stuart's wrote: "I saw a great deal of Bob Stuart in Lake Forest throughout 1941. We argued America First by the hour. He was in my home for Sunday lunch when the news of Pearl Harbor came over the radio. He was in the army within forty-eight hours."

I hadn't thought of the young man since 1941, but it seems to me that his prompt enlistment only pointed up the contrast between reality and the world-picture that the America Firsters tried to impose—like a new breakfast food. And I wasn't second-guessing in 1951, or first-guessing in

understand why what was so plain, in the spring of
1941, in New York and Washington and Lisbon and
London should be so bitterly denied by so large a seg-
ment of the dominant group in this particular city and
region. They appeared to live in a pressurized cabin,
unaffected by the weight of the outside air. It was not
until long afterward that I began to think I understood those men. As much as any unreconstructed
Confederates, the mail-order giants and puffed-fluff
kings have found themselves the leaders of a lost
cause. Their personal fortunes may be great, but the
world has not gone as they willed it. Chicago's bid for
grandeur has failed, and they remain permanently
dissident; whatever happens anywhere else is wrong.
As a matter of fact, most of the men who think of
themselves as leaders have, physically, abandoned
the city out of office hours, and so have most of their

1941. I didn't have to guess, because I had spent the first
year of World War II in France and knew. Wood and Stuart were guessing. General Wood also assured me that for
logistic reasons the United States Army could play no de-
cisive role in a war on the continent of Europe, and I am to
assume therefore, I suppose, that everything I saw happen
there, beginning on the morning of June 6, 1944, never
occurred at all because it was impossible.

assistants. The relatively small white-collar population converges daily on the Loop by rail and at night
leaps over the surrounding sprawl of city wards—
dreary clusters of frame houses and factories—to go
home to suburbs like Oak Park, to the west, and
Evanston, to the north. Upper- and lower-middle
groups commute together, leaving behind them each
night the exiguous skyscraper core and the vast, anonymous pulp of the city, plopped down by the lakeside
like a piece of waterlogged fruit. Chicago after night-
fall is a small city of the rich who have not yet mi-
grated, visitors, and hoodlums, surrounded by a large
expanse of juxtaposed dimnesses.[5]

[5] This is a sensitive point with the migrators. Dr.
Hutchins, leaving the University of Chicago for a job with
the Ford Foundation, recently emptied *his* tail guns in a
series of articles in the Chicago *Daily News,* and he wrote,
among other things: "The leaders of Chicago business and
professional life have moved to the suburbs. Nobody cares
about Chicago."

This aroused an accredited local grandee named Hol-
man D. Pettibone (I invent nothing), president since 1931
of the Chicago Title & Trust Company, and a past president
of the Chicago Association of Commerce and Industry, to
reply, on the first page of that publication: "In making this
statement Dr. Hutchins conveys the impression that when a

By the time of my second visit, I knew at least one Chicago couple. They were a New York woman I had worked with on the old *World* and her husband, a Chicago man, who was employed by a textbook pub- lisher. The city was marvellously dilapidated, they reported when I went to call on them. New York, in retrospect, seemed to the wife a kind of Spotless Town. Chicago was amusing for one year, she said, but after the arrival of the baby she was expecting, they would move to Evanston, which has a Bahai temple, Northwestern University, and no saloons.[6]

When I returned again to Chicago, in 1949, it was

citizen takes up his residence in a suburb he loses all inter- est in Chicago; he fails to carry his share of public respon- sibility; he is some sort of a disloyal renegade. As a subur- ban resident, I disagree."

The fiercest epistolary defenders of Chicago live in places like Winnetka and Lake Forest.

[6] My Winnetka admirer and another woman have both signalized my dislocation of the Bahai temple. North- western is in Evanston, all right, but the Bahai temple is in the next town, Wilmette. No saloons are in both of them. "It happens to be in Wilmette, not Evanston, for all your erudite eastern enlightenment!" It is humiliating.

with the soon regretted design of settling down there for some time. So did various of Hakluyt's venturers, on one voyage sighting a coast afar and on a second putting ashore a boat's crew who shot an Indian with a gold ring in his nose, return a third time for a full-scale settlement, with women, hens, and demiculverins, only to perish of shipwreck, arrows, or malaria. On this voyage, I took with me a wife and stepdaughter, and by then I had a considerable circle of Chicago acquaintances—a psychiatrist, whom I had come to know in North Africa during the war, and his wife; a war correspondent, retired, and *his* wife; the textbook people, who had moved to the aseptic suburb of Evanston; and an assortment of others, whom my wife and I had met at cocktail parties in New York. A friend's friend had found for us, after weeks of intelligence work, a furnished apartment. (Housing was tighter in Chicago than even in Washington, we were informed.) We had abandoned a New York apartment, and it struck us that the one the Chicagoan had turned up for us was incomparably more elegant, though far less comfortable than the one we had left. It was on the Gold Coast, two short blocks from the Lake, in a building of which the upper floors command a lacustrine vista that increases rentals. Unfortunately, we were on a lower floor. It was a sixteen-story coöperative building with two apartments on each floor, and the woman just above us, with whom our landlord had left the key, said it was as friendly as an old-time boarding house. "All the apartments are laid out just alike," she told us, "and that makes it homey, because no matter whose apartment you're in, you know where everything is. Last New Year's Eve, eleven of us got together and gave a party in all our eleven apartments, one above the other. One apartment was South American, with a rumba band, and another was Wild West, with a square-dance caller, and another French, with an accordionist, and you just took the elevator from one to another, and lay where you fell."

The woman across the hall was even friendlier. On being introduced, she suggested to my wife that after we had moved in, we leave our door on the latch and she would leave hers, so we could wander in and out like one big family. We ducked that one, and laid ourselves open to an imputation of Eastern snobbishness. It is uncertain, however, whether the woman wanted us to act upon her proposal. A transplanted Philadelphian we met later said that at his first Chicago parties everybody he met insisted they must get together again within a week. None ever called. "It's just a way of talking they have," he said. "I don't think they're very warm. They mix less than they say they will, and perhaps less than they think they do. They're not given to meeting friends in restaurants, which means that their social repertory is fixed by their facilities for entertaining. A family able to manage two dinners for six guests each every month, for instance, will soon find itself limited to friendship with six couples, for each couple will invite it back every month, and the next month it starts all over again. This means a snug schedule, and the only way to break it without making two enemies is to leave town." [7]

[7] This statement apparently aroused passionate resentment. One of my wife's best women friends in Chicago, while challenging little in the piece, wrote: "You know that everybody knows more than six couples." The woman in question, however, has a big house, and so have most of her friends. It is therefore probable that she maintains relations with seven couples, or eight if one husband and one wife are midgets.

I checked on this social impression with a man I met

in Chicago last May, an outlander like myself, but engaged in business there. He said he had temporarily reversed the usual outward drift by moving his family back from a suburb into Chicago. (It had been easy for him because he was a hotel man. He could therefore shunt them around among vacant suites.) "We had to move in to get away from the little circuit of people we knew there," he said. "After a while we can move out to some other suburb and meet some other people it will take us a couple of years to get sick of. I figure there are enough suburbs to last us until the youngest kid goes away to college, and then my wife and I can move into a double and bath and pretend we're transients."

Because of this roundrobinnical social life, a family can live in any suburb and have as many friends as in the city itself, or in the city and know as few people as if it inhabited the smallest suburb. It eliminates one of the great pleasures of urban living and spreads boredom as evenly as cream cheese on a drugstore sandwich.

At Her Feet

the Slain Deer

···

WHEN I was in Chicago a couple of months ago, a friend of mine who lives out there and manufactures roulette wheels, craps layouts, wheels of fortune for carnivals, shuffleboard games, and juke boxes—he looks like Samuel Seabury and is considered an elder statesman of the amusement-devices business—told me a story about a simple fellow called Porky, whom the boys at Clark and Madison enlisted to shove synthetic diamonds. My friend's father was a successful gambler of the nineties who invested his savings in real estate and got cleaned out. To recoup his fortunes, he began manufacturing gambling equipment. His son carries on with the roulette and craps lines because they are a family tradition; he continues to turn out a well-balanced roulette wheel as an exercise in filial piety, for the real money now is in coarser ware. Chicago is the center of coin-machine manufacture, including coin-operated gambling games; it accounts for twenty per cent of the nation's total volume. "Most of our stuff is sold to fraternal organizations and churches," my friend says. "I always advise them to stay away from roulette and craps. They're hard games for amateurs to run, and a gambler might take them. What they want is a nice wheel of fortune with plenty of flash."

"It was around 1905," my friend began when he told me the Porky story. "Some guy in Germany had invented these rocks that would meet about every test for a natural diamond, except there was just something about them that would give them away to an expert. When they were mounted in rings, they were even

harder to tell from the real thing. So the boys were un-loading them on pawnbrokers. A pawnbroker takes a quick look at a ring, guesses it's worth around two hundred dollars, and offers to lend maybe fifteen on it. If he was going to buy it, it would make a differ-ence exactly what the stone was worth, so he would size it up more closely. But he didn't think he was going to buy it. So one of the boys would walk into a hock shop as if he needed a stake in a hurry, leave the ring, take the fifteen, and never go back. When it became the pawnbroker's property, he would find the stone was worth seventy-five cents. Porky had the kind of dumb face that wouldn't make a broker suspicious, and the boys were trying to give him courage to go into this dodge. 'You can't hardly tell them from the real thing,' they were telling him, and giving him reasons why. 'Stop, fellows!' Porky says. 'I don't want to hear anything more. When I go into that store, I want to be-lieve they *are* real.' "

My friend also told me how a fair-sized industry, the manufacture of the fruit-symbol slot machines known as one-armed bandits, was captured for Chicago. The first slot machines, he said, were electrically operated, and were always getting out of order. Then a machinist named Charlie Fey, in San Francisco, hit upon the notion of a machine that operated by gravity, and, using that principle, built the first fruit-symbol machine. He sold it to a saloonkeeper, and it made such a hit that he received more orders than he could fill working by himself in his basement shop. Fey got in touch with a manufacturer in Chicago, who agreed to make the machines for him. You can't patent a gambling device, but before sending the plans for his machine to the Chicago man Fey exacted a promise from the fellow that the first five hundred machines he produced would be shipped to him, as the inventor, in San Francisco, where he had orders for most of them. The Chicago manufacturer put the machine in production, and shipped the first five hundred to Fey, all right, but routed them by ordinary freight via his agents in Halifax, Tampa, Banff, Chattanooga, and a few dozen other places, and while they were en route, he sold the second, third, and fourth five hundred, a lot of them in California. Chicago has been the center of the one-armed-bandit business ever since.

Faith like Porky's and imaginative enterprise like the slot-machine manufacturer's are ingredients lacking in contemporary Chicago. When, in 1857, a Chicago *Tribune* editorialist wrote of this city, "The sign is still onward until the last rival in the race for greatness is left behind," the chances are he meant it. So, probably, did another *Tribune* man, who wrote, thirty-six years later, during the Columbian Exposition, "In her white tent like Minnehaha, the arrow maker's daughter, stood Chicago yesterday morning and gazed out on a sapphire lake, under a blue and cloudless sky, and her Hiawatha, her World Lover, came to her, and laid at her feet the slain deer, the tribute of universal admiration and love." At the world's feet, Chicago, in return, laid a butchered hog. The city was certified the third biggest in the United States by the census of 1880, and the second biggest by that of 1890, having more than doubled its population in the intervening decade. The figures were 503,000 in 1880 and

1,100,000 ten years later. Chicago's relative position has remained the same ever since; Los Angeles is now a serious threat to its hold on even second place.[1] The hopes for all-round preëminence, to come as an automatic bonus for being biggest, have faded, too. Still, the habit of purely quantitative thinking persists. The city consequently has the personality of a man brought up in the expectation of a legacy who has learned in middle age that it will never be his.

The kind of buccaneering drive that won the slot-machine industry for the city has been lacking since a date that is hard to fix definitely but that preceded

---

[1] The population of Chicago in 1940 was 3,396,000; of Los Angeles, 1,504,000. The census of 1950 showed Chicago with 3,606,000, a gain of about 6 per cent; Los Angeles with 1,957,000, a gain of 30 per cent. If population growth continues at these rates the two cities will be neck-and-neck in about twenty-five years. It isn't certain that Los Angeles will continue to grow that fast, of course. It was upon precisely such a calculation that the Chicagoans of 1890 based their hopes of overtaking London and New York.

Philadelphia, by the way, still clung to third place in 1950, with 2,064,000, a gain of 133,000 over 1940.

Chicago, as of today, is the seventh biggest city in the world, outranked only by London, New York, Shanghai, Tokyo, Berlin, and Moscow. It has a big edge over Paris in population.

the rise of the automobile. "Chicago could have had the automobile industry if Chicago money had gone out after it," a Chicago stockbroker assured me. "We're nearer than Detroit to both iron ore and coal, and we had the greatest supply of skilled and unskilled labor in America when Detroit was still a small city. But the big boys let it go by default; they didn't want an industry in here that would dwarf them. The arteries had already hardened." The financial community has accepted its secondary position. All the Midwest Stock Exchange aspires to, its president, James E. Day, told me, is a top minor-league rating, specializing in Midwestern issues of not quite national magnitude. Many stocks listed on the big board in Wall Street are also bought and sold on the Chicago exchange, of course, but it is like play away from the race track. When a Chicago corporation—International Harvester, for example—is so big that it is listed on the New York Stock Exchange, the New York volume of transactions in its shares exceeds the Chicago volume by as much as twelve to one. According to some Chicago businessmen with whom I have talked, the city's two great banks—the First National and the Continental—which flex their two-and-a-half-billion-dollar muscles in trade publications, no longer undertake ventures on the grand scale without the assent of the still biggest banks in the East. The old nineteenth-century dream of making Chicago a great port, from which ships would carry grain and ore direct to Europe, has subsided to such an extent that the *Tribune* last year editorially opposed the St. Lawrence Seaway scheme because it might bring a lot of foreign shipping to the Great Lakes. Foreign ships, the *Tribune* feared, might drive American lake steamers from the Canadian trade. From "Let me at him!" the city's cry has changed to "Hold him offa me!"

The collective sense of disappointment is evident in the utterances of the town's tutelary deity, Colonel Robert R. McCormick, the *Tribune's* publisher. The Colonel was a youth in the era of the city's greatest expectations (he was born in 1880), and the few scores of millions of dollars that he has been able to add to the family fortunes since have been unable to reconcile him to his position as first citizen of a not-quite metropolis. Even the circulation of the New York *Daily News*, more than twice that of the *Tribune*, must annoy him sometimes with its constant reminder of status, although he inherited control of the *News* after the death of Captain Joseph Medill Patterson, his first cousin. It is too late for the Colonel to leave Chicago now. The office of tutelary deity is not elective. The god just sets himself up, and then starts pitching thunderbolts at anybody who laughs. Colonel McCormick hurls a delightfully reverberant thunderbolt, flavored with sassafras. When, for instance, the Montreal *Star* recently took exception to one of his dicta, the *Tribune* countered with an editorial headed "The Kicked Dog Howls," which read, in part, "The Montreal *Star*, howling like a kicked dog, has endeavored to reply to a radio speech by the publisher of the *Tribune* on Canada and Canadian-American relations. Since the *Star* could not reply with candor to his remarks on the efforts of the Union Nowers and Rhodes scholars to destroy the sovereignty of Canada along with that of the United States—because the *Star* is deeply involved in that movement—it adopted more devious tactics." I do not know whether the *Star*, itself no maiden's sigh, responded with an editorial headed "The Stuck Pig Squeals." The Colonel would not have blenched, in any case. He is accustomed to think of himself as the man most feared by the British Empire, which for him begins at the Hudson River.

The opportunity to view a tutelary deity should never be passed up by an explorer, so during the winter of 1949–50, while my wife and I were living in Chicago, I arranged to attend one of the weekly ceremonies at which the Colonel manifests himself to his people. These are the broadcasts of what is known as "The Chicago Theatre of the Air," from nine to ten every Saturday evening over WGN (for World's Greatest Newspaper), the *Tribune's* radio station. They are put on in a broadcasting hall, which is sometimes also called the Chicago Theatre of the Air and adjoins the Tribune Tower, an example of Wedding-Cake Gothic that the Colonel considers the equal of the Taj Mahal, although to me it has a look of incompleteness. The architect, I have always thought, should have finished it off with a gigantic double scoop of ice cream, topped by an illuminated cherry.

Among Chicagoans of more than grade-school education, there is a disposition to deprecate the Colonel, just as in Periclean Athens there doubtless was an intellectual clique that made discreet jokes about owls. Some of the scoffers among my acquaintances in Chicago greeted my project of attending one of his séances with exclamations of disbelief, like New Yorkers learning that an out-of-towner wants to visit the Statue of Liberty. "I never read the *Tribune*," "I never believe anything I read in the *Tribune*," "I read the *Tribune* just for laughs," and "Colonel McCormick never wins an election" are four passwords used by enlightened Chicagoans to establish their affranchisement. The Colonel, nonetheless, has been the chief molder of the city since the nearly simultaneous, though unrelated, withdrawals of Al Capone and Samuel Insull, twenty years ago.

I was not to be dissuaded. Tickets for the broadcast, I was informed when I telephoned the radio station, must be applied for by mail at least four weeks in advance. I overcame this difficulty, which I had scarcely anticipated, by appealing to the WGN press agent. My surprise at the demand for seats arose because I had been preparing for the occasion by reading the texts of some of the Colonel's previous broadcasts, transcripts of which are available, free, to anybody who drops in at the Tribune Tower and asks for them. Most of the broadcasts were on historical topics, like "Nathanael Greene, Strategist," "John Paul Jones (I and II)," and "The Boston Massacre," not to be confused with the 1929 Saint Valentine's Day Massacre in Chicago. Others were on international affairs, such as the importance of the Panama Canal, where, Colonel McCormick told his WGN audience in 1947, he had caught Trygve Lie "spying out the land." The Colonel commented at that time, "I am glad it is not Henry Luce, who could spy it out just as well and not be so obvious." Colonel McCormick is an authority on espionage; his best script purely from the point of view of entertainment, I thought, was one entitled "Mata Hari's Innocence." It began: "Mata Hari has so long been known as a spy that it is too late to change her undeserved reputation. This is the truth of the matter." The climax of the truth of the matter was:

> Mata Hari also was tried as a spy. Malvy, reputed to be her lover, persuaded her not to confess or testify, saying he would take care of her.

When she was convicted and condemned to death he again persuaded her not to confess or testify, guaranteeing that the guns of the firing squad would not contain bullets. He told her that as an actress she could fall as if dead, that she would be picked up and put into a coffin, and at the cemetery she would be transferred into an automobile and driven to Spain. The simple woman believed him. She went before the firing squad at the fortress of Vincennes. All of the rifles were loaded with bullets. She fell dead, was taken to the cemetery and buried. Her secret was buried with her and she has borne to this day the false accusation of being a spy.

Another script, apparently the Colonel's favorite, since he repeats it on an average of once every three months (the *Tribune* prints it in full each time, as it does all his broadcasts), was about the 1st Division, in which, I knew, he had served briefly in the First World War. The peroration went: "March on, then, First Division! March over the sunny hills of France; march thru the flaming towns of Picardy, up the shell-swept slopes of Lorraine, thru the gas-filled forest of Argonne—on to everlasting glory." I liked it, but I didn't think that anybody who had been in some other division would care to hear it more than once a season.

I soon learned that in assuming there would not be a capacity turnout to listen to such oratory I had underestimated the Colonel, an error into which it is easy to fall. Among other things, "The Chicago Theatre of the Air" presents condensed versions of musical shows like "The Student Prince" and "No, No, Nanette," and the Colonel's speeches are usually sandwiched in between the well-buttered slices of divertissement, so that to hear the second half of the show the studio audience has to sit through the homily.[2] The attraction on the evening I was to attend was Rudolf Friml's "The Vagabond King," running fore and aft of a talk by the Colonel on "The American Navy." "The Vagabond King," as you probably remember, is the musical comedy containing the song

[2] An anonymous Chicagoan, thinking I missed the point, typed on a postcard: "People don't listen to hear McCormick's asinine speeches. They want to hear Nancy Carr's singing. You know: music!"

about "And to hell with BurgunDEE!" It tells how François Villon is made ruler of France for a day, after which he is to be executed, and how he saves France and wins a fair lady's hand and escapes unscathed.

The Chicago Theatre of the Air looks very much like the usual broadcasting studio, with a stage but no scenery, and a couple of hundred comfortable seats, and it was full when I arrived there, a good fifteen minutes before the performance. My fellow-spectators in the audience were well-dressed, suburban-looking people (the system of application by mail allows the studio officials to pick guests with nice addresses), quite evidently grateful for the opportunity to see something resembling theatre without paying for it. There is, by the way, little opportunity to see theatre in Chicago even if you do pay for it. As a theatrical center, it is outclassed by Oslo, which has a population of four hundred thousand.

The members of the cast, in evening clothes of various degrees of formality, were seated about the stage —rabble of Paris and nobles of Louis XI's court dressed out of the same department stores. There was a good-sized orchestra, as well as a female chorus in delft-blue dresses. At the beginning of the show, the master of ceremonies-*cum*-narrator introduced the performers, none of whose names I remember. There were two François Villons—one in tails, who sang, and a black-tie one, who spoke lines. The narrator had some very poetic things to say about eyes. "The lowering dusk with flaring eyes of impending war" was one I think I noted on my cuff, but, my shirt having been washed before I transcribed the notes, I can't be sure that it wasn't "glaring eyes." One I am sure of, though, is "The King's eyes betrayed his evil scheme."

"Fear not, milady," the black-tie Villon would say. "My men have taken over this balcony en masse." Then the white-tie Villon would step to the microphone and intone "Only a Rose." The girls in delft blue would back him up. I liked it fine.

Presently, however, my attention was diverted to a control booth at the left side of the stage. Through its glass window I could see the profile of a tall old man with a long gray face and puffy eyes. He wore an unpointed gray mustache designed to break the sweep of an overlong upper lip, and he looked rather as if he were about to cry. I attributed this to the effect of Rudolf Friml's music, but it was more probably, I ascertained a little later, the result of a cold in the head. The old man first looked at the audience, as if counting the all-paper house. Some chamberlain's head would have rolled, I suppose, if he had descried any empty seats, but probably a platoon of spares— wives and children of *Tribune* editors—is held in reserve for such emergencies. He then turned an appreciative grandfatherly eye on the young woman singing the part of Huguette, the girl of the people—she was wearing a strapless silver evening gown with an ermine thing around her neck—and at last concentrated on reading over a typed script he was holding in his hand. This, I heard afterward, is a precaution he has scrupulously observed ever since a time when, reading a script he had not previously seen, he was overcome by emotion and burst into sobs before his audience. The script that so moved him was about the scalping of a pioneer mother by an Indian who had got drunk on rum purveyed to him by an English nobleman.

Precisely as the studio clock showed twenty-five

minutes past the hour, with the pack in full melodious cry ("Onwood! Onwood! On ta face tha ff—"), the narrator stepped to the mike, swallowing a fifteenth-century accent, and said, "We will now hear an address on 'The American Navy,' by Colonel Robert Rutherford McCormick, publisher of the Chicago *Tribune*." The old man walked out of the booth and onto the stage. I thought I could see on the faces around me a certain resentment at the interruption, but the faces' owners applauded politely. The singers closed their mouths as unobtrusively as possible. The speech was the kind of résumé that could have been culled from a couple of public-library books in an hour, embellished by a few digs at Great Britain. The Colonel read it completely without expression, pausing only to sniffle. In fifteen minutes, he got the American Navy out of the Bonhomme Richard era and into that of the internal-combustion engine, and finally "guid-id miss-siles." As he finished reading each sheet, he let it flutter to the floor, and as he dropped the last one, the conductor was already giving the orchestra the come-on. The Colonel had talked more slowly than usual, because of his cold, and the Duke of Bur-

gundy waited impatiently at the gates of Paris. "Onwood! Onwood! On ta face tha foe!" shrieked the
blue ladies as the lecturer moved toward the wings,
and the members of the audience again looked
happy.[3]

[3] Another, disaffected, Chicagoan who did sign, has
written:

> I felt obligated to express my sympathy at the
> fact you were so unfortunate as to see just a second
> rate performance of Col. McCormick reading a speech.
> Somewhere in the years between 1943 and 1947
> I was forced, or shall I say strongly encouraged, to at-
> tend a special performance of the Chicago Theatre of
> the Air presented at Medinah Temple in honor of the
> Reserve Officers' Training Corps (ROTC), a special
> love of the Colonel's.
> That evening, in uniform, we arrived at the Tem-
> ple somewhat early, and were seated close to the large
> stage, whence I was able to see (and resist the temp-
> tation of throwing a spitball at) the Colonel.
> The Chicago High School ROTC is close to the
> heart of the Colonel, as he told us that evening, for
> he was, for all intents and purposes, its founder. It is
> to the credit of the Army that our instructors gave the
> Congress more credit than the Colonel, but perhaps they
> knew who paid their salaries. On the selfsame evening
> the Colonel also informed us (he was lecturing on
> things military) that he had saved the U.S. from Ca-
> nadian invasion during World War I, and that he had

. . .

It was typical of the Colonel to appear and read his speech despite his cold. He would not let his people down. The cultural wool fat in which he has chosen to embed his talks characterizes his own taste. The *Trib-*

invented the machine gun. As oldtime Chicagoans, we had heard all this before, but we listened respectfully.

The really entertaining part of the show, however, was the manner in which the speech was delivered.

In contrast to the way he was sandwiched in at your performance, in this instance he came on within the first fifteen minutes of the show. Wearing a dinner jacket, he was accompanied by a pleasant young man who carried his speech, a glass, and a pitcher of water. The Colonel apparently wasn't quite up to snuff, for he had a cane in each hand, though they appeared to be merely surplus, for he stood quite erect. As he would finish a page, the young man would turn the pages, and when he wanted a drink, the young man would pour the water, hold a cane, and the Colonel would drink. I would give a better report of what he said if I hadn't been so engrossed in these mechanics.

The Colonel's fortitude when duty's to be done is well illustrated in this reminiscence, as well as his knack of being prepared for all emergencies. Two canes are better than one, even when you don't lean on either, because if you did happen to lean on one it might break.

une recently ran a front-page cartoon, in color, labelled "The Three (Dis) Graces"—"Depraved Art" (an obvious foreigner, in a beret and smock, carrying a smeared canvas intended to represent an abstract painting), "Sedition" (an unattractive lady of Levantine features, wearing a red Liberty cap), and "Pornographic Literature" (another female, round-faced and bespectacled, hauling a manuscript from a garbage can). Art, according to the *Tribune's* canon, has been depraved since Landseer, literature has been pornographic since James Whitcomb Riley, and sedition begins with a wish to redraft the Illinois Constitution of 1870, which, in effect, bars a state income tax. The Colonel's conviction that the world is going to the dogs antedates the New Deal; it was Herbert Hoover upon whom he made his famous pronouncement "The man won't do." His pessimism weighs heavily on his city.

It is a miasmic influence, discernible in the conviction of every Chicagoan that he is being done. Plays at Chicago theatres, for example, are always locally assumed to be inferior versions of the New York productions, or, if they *are* the New York produc-

tions, with original casts intact, the actors are presumed to be giving inferior performances. Taking an
interest in the Chicago theatre, therefore, is regarded
as naïve, as my wife and I discovered when, attending a party shortly after our arrival in the city, we
innocently inquired what shows in town were worth
seeing. Chicagoans with the price of airplane tickets
do their theatregoing here in New York, where, along
with people from Boise, Chillicothe, and Winnemucca,
they pay such exorbitant premiums for tickets to hits
that most of the natives never see them. It is not considered smart to admit having seen any play in Chicago, because this implies either (a) that you haven't
seen the *real* play or (b) that you haven't the airplane
fare or (c), and possibly worst of all, that you are in-
different to nuances and might, therefore, just as well
go back to Fond du Lac, Wisconsin, where you went
to high school. Whether this approach to the theatre originated with the *Tribune*, whose current critic,
Claudia Cassidy, is its high priestess; with those pro-
ducers who have in fact sent out bad shows; or with
the airlines' sales-promotion departments, I do not
know. But it interested me that the Chicagoans who

60

do their playgoing in New York say they never take the *Tribune* seriously. What I suspect they mean is that they never take the *Tribune* seriously consciously. While my wife and I were in Chicago, a company of "Death of a Salesman" put in an appearance and proved to be, according to a reliable friend of mine who had seen the play in New York, better than the original company; the show lasted for only a hundred and seventy-five performances and closed in midseason. In this particular case, I believe, Miss Cassidy had praised, but the Chicago theatre has fallen below the point where an individual review can do much for a show.

With the best-heeled and most knowing slice of the potential Chicago audience thus eliminated, actors have become aware of a curious sensation when playing the place. An actress who appeared there in "The Madwoman of Chaillot" during my stay said that she had a feeling the audience meant to be kind, but that it always laughed in the wrong places. Another large portion of the potential audience is incommunicado overnight in the suburbs, to which train service after commuting hours is awful beyond a Long Island

Railroad trustee's fondest vision of what it is feasible to get away with. (The suburbanites go in for amateur theatricals coached by professionals; a young man of my acquaintance became the central figure of a taut situation in Glenview by putting on "Springtime for Henry," the antiseptic 1931 chestnut. The local Catholic priest found it scandalous.) And those great, silent, though densely populated, spaces, the outlying city wards, are peopled by frequenters of neighborhood movies who are now turning to television.

Whoever started the ball rolling, it's under the truck now. A summary of the season of 1950–51 by Miss Cassidy herself lists twenty-three attractions, which played a total of a hundred and fifty-two weeks at seven theatres. The most successful was the national company of "South Pacific," and the three next were, in order, a revival of "Diamond Lil" and holdover-from-the-previous-season runs of "Lend an Ear" and "Two Blind Mice." Among the rest were "Ti-Coq," something called "Mike McCauley," which ran four performances, and "Borscht Capades." During the season, there were seldom more than four theatres open concurrently, and sometimes only three. "Look over your shoulder, if you can bear it, and contemplate what purported to be our season," Miss Cassidy wrote last June before taking off on a three-month tour of Europe to see some shows and hear some music. (She is the *Tribune's* critic of music and the dance, as well.) The lot of drama critics in Chicago is an enviable one, for they are expected to visit New York to see the new shows; they see eight or ten a week, at a glob, just like out-of-town paying customers. Their advantage over their New York colleagues is that while working they live on an expense account. Looked at from this angle, nothing could be more disastrous for Chicago theatre critics than a revival of the Chicago theatre.

Chicago's wariness extends to women's clothes, I discovered through my wife. Women who wouldn't think of going to a show in Chicago told her they wouldn't think of buying a dress in a Chicago store, either. New York stores like Saks Fifth Avenue and Bonwit Teller have Chicago branches, but these women distrust them, too. They suspect that the clothes at the Chicago Saks and Bonwit differ from

those at the New York Saks and Bonwit, having, pre-
sumably, been chosen in accordance with some patron-
izing New York notion of Chicago taste. They circum-
vent this presumed strategy by buying clothes during
their New York trips, on afternoons when there are no
matinées. My wife thought this remarkable, because
she herself found a lot of dresses she wanted in Chicago. It's a field in which I have no competence. Only
the repetition of the motif of distrust interested me.[4]

[4] A correspondent suggests an interesting but discour-
aging theory about this shopping.

"The Chicago taste for clothes is different from New
York," he writes. "So actually it makes little difference
where Chicago buys, for inevitably their taste will predom-
inate. I suspect that every New York store has clothes for
Chicagoans. But, except for the labels, the styles are the
same as those on sale on the shores of Lake Michigan—
flamboyant, scrumptious, frabjous. You can turn that picture around, too. New York women would be dressed as
well no matter where they bought, even in Chicago."

This would explain how my wife found clothes she
wanted in the Chicago stores, but the double treachery it
ascribes to New York retailers—stocking Chicago-taste
clothes for sale to Chicago women at both ends of the air-
line, is a little hard to swallow. It is a theory the passenger
departments of the airlines must explode, for if it stands
up, the intercity fares expended by shoppers are demon-
strably a waste. And, after all, how is the New York ven-

Opera has succumbed completely to the lack of faith. The gloriously sonorous old Auditorium, home of Chicago's own opera companies from 1910 until the late twenties, when the monster Civic Opera House,

deuse to know that the customer is from Chicago, so that she can bring out the frabjous little number or the scrumptious model? My correspondent has an answer for that, too, but I do not believe him.

"Chicago ladies apply makeup to their cheeks with equal abandon," he writes. "In New York the women gild the lily lightly."

I found Chicago women pretty and they looked well-dressed to me. It just interested me that so many didn't *think* they were well-dressed unless they had bought their clothes somewhere else.

A very smart (in both senses of the word) Chicago woman I know looked around her in a New York restaurant a few years ago and said, "There's something about New York women that simply makes me feel awkward." The restaurant, as it happens, is little more than a saloon, and the "New York women" were for the most part newspaper reporters not long out of smaller places than Chicago. They were wearing, I should think, ready-made clothes of brands the visitor wouldn't look at in Marshall Field's, since they would be in some kind of a popular-prices department. Her feeling about them had no objective basis.

Frenchwomen cast something of the same spell over female visitors from across the Channel. WAF officers who had felt themselves belles in London would walk into cafés on Wacker Drive, was opened, stands disused and out of repair. The Civic Opera House itself is occupied only now and then, by such travelling attractions as "Peter Pan" and the Sadler's Wells Ballet; the Metropolitan gave four performances there last May after the close of its New York season. The Chicago Symphony bears up, or has borne up so far, under a constant fire of criticism based on its supposed inferiority to the Boston, the Philadelphia, and the Philharmonic. That it is a pleasant orchestra to listen to when it plays good music is seldom mentioned in print or over cocktails.

The drawbacks of the first-or-nothing psychology in a city that, it now seems certain, will never be first, impress a visitor to the dejected macrocosm gradually, one by one.

Chicago is the country's foremost printing town,

---

in Paris after the Liberation and for the first time in their lives become conscious of their wrist joints. Yet the competition might not be much.

It's a hoodoo, which might be mathematically expressed: NYW: CW: FW: EW.

but little publishing is done there. Giant printeries turn out billions of telephone directories, railroad timetables, and copies of *Time* and *Life,* but the most talked-about national magazine edited in Chicago is the spry Negro monthly *Ebony,* with its affiliates *Jet* (the size of *Quick*) and *Tan Confessions* (rather like *True Confessions*).[5] Even *Esquire* has moved its editorial offices to New York, where most of the writers

[5] Most staff members, however, feel ill at ease in Chicago, and there is hot competition for out-of-town assignments. A couple of them explained to me, awhile ago, that Negro Chicago is like its white counterpart, a bit heavy and materialistic. Writers don't rate as high as they do in Harlem, and all the Negro stars of the entertainment world make their headquarters in New York or Hollywood. Chicago's Negroes have a different recent geographical origin from New York's, they pointed out—most of them have come north along the line of the Mississippi River and the Illinois Central Railroad, from Alabama, Mississippi, Tennessee, and Arkansas, while New York's Negroes are mainly from the South Atlantic states, with a strong leavening of West Indians. The general level of Negro education is lowest in the lower Mississippi states, and the mass immigration into Chicago is on the whole newer than that into New York. "But Chicago's a better town for a Negro to make a living in, if he could find someplace to live," my *Ebony* men conceded. "There are more jobs in heavy industry than there are in New York."

are. Nor has the city one major publisher of general books. There is, though, Rand, McNally, which specializes in atlases and "Kon-Tiki," and a new firm, the Henry Regnery Company, which makes a specialty of anti-Roosevelt "revelations."

There are four newspapers of any consequence in Chicago, of which only the *Tribune* is, in its own peculiar way, exceptional. Its rival in the morning field, Marshall Field's *Sun-Times,* is a tabloid, ordinarily Democratic in national politics (though it has just endorsed General Eisenhower), cleanly edited, and not without enterprise, but, for mechanical reasons, cursed by limited space, so its out-of-town and foreign coverage is uncomfortably concise. It sometimes raises a great row with stories about local political graft, which have a circulation value, since the contemplation of municipal corruption is always gratifying to Chicagoans. They are helpless to do anything about it, but they like to know it is on a big scale. This is a point the *Tribune* seems to have forgotten in recent years. Although Chicago municipal graft is necessarily Democratic, since the city's government is Democratic, it is the *Sun-Times,* rather than the

Tribune, that gets indignant. There is, indeed, a widespread belief that the *Tribune* is on good terms with the Democratic city machine; certainly it reserves its foam-flecked-lips editorials for Governor Adlai E. Stevenson, a liberal Democrat who was nominated, and won, in 1948, when the state leaders thought they could not stem "the Dewey tide" with a Party hack. Dewey, in the same fashion, is responsible for the liberal Democratic United States Senator Paul H. Douglas, who was nominated in the same campaign.

The *Tribune's* circulation, which stood at 1,076,-000 in 1946, has dropped off to 925,000, while the *Sun-Times* has established a solid and apparently profitable circulation of almost 600,000 where no morning circulation except the *Tribune's* existed in 1941, when Field started his paper, as the *Sun.* (He later acquired the Chicago *Times,* an afternoon paper, and made his present newspaper out of the pair.) In Chicago proper, the *Tribune* has only 60,000 more readers than the newcomer, the rest of its superiority lying in its suburban and out-of-town circulation. The *Sun-Times* buys the New York *Herald Tribune's* foreign and Washington services (it has a Washington bureau of its own, too) but hasn't the space to print more than a small part of them. Its limit is ninety-six tabloid pages, and advertisements, features, photographs, and funnies reduce its news space below the intellectual subsistence level even when it prints the full ninety-six with a proud house ad announcing that *x* columns of paid advertising have had to be refused. In contrast, the unlimited bales of advertising the *Tribune* carries are its greatest circulation asset. As long as large masses of women pine to know what goes on in the department stores, Colonel McCormick's editorial policies won't hurt his paper much. The growth of the *Sun-Times*, however, is evidence of the resentment he has built up. The only alternative to the Colonel's dream world is the *Sun-Times'* world—neat, if limited.

In the afternoon field, there are the *Herald-American*, a Hearst paper that is like every other Hearst paper on earth, and the *Daily News*, a good-looking, fundamentally negative newspaper owned by John S. Knight, who also owns papers in Detroit, Miami, and his home town, Akron, Ohio. (As I write this, I learn that the *Sun-Times* has just expanded its operations and is now publishing on a round-the-clock basis, but it is too early to say how this policy will be received.) Literate Chicagoans speak wistfully of the time when the *News,* under the ownership before last, was a "great newspaper," by which they mean that it was Chicago's own and amusing to read. Right now, it is neither. Even so, it has been moving ahead in the vacuum left in the afternoon field by the *Herald-American,* which is aimed at the intellectual level of a slightly subnormal strip-tease girl.

The reader who stays on Chicago newspapers exclusively for a month (I made the experiment) feels, on seeing his first New York *Times* or *Herald Tribune* after the ordeal, like a diver returning to the light. A year of this underwater swimming and he must surely have forgotten what it was like on the surface. In this subaqueous atmosphere, at least two columnists move like relatively big fish. They are Irv Kupcinet, of the *Sun-Times,* and Sydney J. Harris, of the *News.*

Kupcinet, generally known as Kup, is a large, powerful man, a former professional football player, whose chief material is the interview with the Hollywood movie star on his or her way through Chicago to New York or the New York stage performer on his or her way through Chicago to Hollywood. The arrival of these celebrities by train is a sign that they desire to be interviewed, since otherwise they would simply fly over. On getting to town, they check in at one of the two Ambassador Hotels, which stand on opposite sides of North State Street and are connected by a passage under the pavement. They post themselves at tables in the Pump Room of the Ambassador East in order to be "run into" by Kupcinet and by his imitators on the other three papers. ("Ran into Charles Boyer last night in the Pump Room. . . .") The pretext for the actor's presence in Chicago is the layover between trains; the traveller arriving in Chicago must get out of his incoming train and station and travel across town to an outgoing train, in another station. (He sometimes has the privilege of staying in his car, if he wishes, but this involves several dull hours as the car is shunted from one railroad yard to another.) The late Ernest L. Byfield, a partner in several Chicago hotels, founded the Pump Room in the confident expectation that the railroads would never

improve their service. When, shortly after the war, Robert R. Young, the chairman of the board of the Chesapeake & Ohio Railway, began a campaign of newspaper advertisements urging through passenger trains ("A hog can cross America without changing trains—but YOU can't"), Mr. Byfield, always a profoundly sad man, grew even sadder. "If they ever have through trains, *nobody* will stop here," he said. "How could a guy admit he was taking an extra day just so he could happen to be run into by columnists from four papers with a total circulation of a couple of million and nothing to write about?" The well and gratuitously advertised presence of the celebrities keeps the Pump Room crowded with less illustrious but more profitable guests, who come in the hope of recognizing the current attraction. Incidentally, the Pump Room serves as a center for the spread of sophistication. "It was here in this place I first ate snails," I heard a man say there.

I saw a more indigenous brand of knowingness displayed at the Sirloin Room of the Stockyards Inn during the run of the annual International Livestock Show and Chicago Horse Show, which flourish concurrently each November. The chairs in the Sirloin Room are covered with red-and-white cow fur, in the interior-decorator manner. A party of stockmen came in, high on a distillation of the stuff they feed their cows, and one of them wanted a *black* cow fur to sit on. "I want to sit on an Angus," he bawled. "I won't sit on a Hereford." He was loyal to the breed he made his money on.

The International, by the way, is a congenial affair, perhaps the pleasantest on the Chicago calendar. The New York Horse Show makes the mistake of treating the horse as a creature apart, instead of showing him in a setting of other domestic animals. The International has hogs, sheep, cattle, and, I think, rabbits for you to go next door and look at during the harness classes, and the Horse Show part of the enterprise gives working horses a turn in the ring—eighteen-hand Clydesdales, and range-cutting horses ridden by cowboys. It has more of a circus atmosphere than New York's, first because it smells stronger and second because it is jammed with 4-H-Club kids in from the real Middle West for corn- or calf-judging contests. The added spectacular attraction, when I was there, was also authentically circusy—maneuvers by a club of Midwestern Arabian horse fanciers, dressed like mounted nobles of the Mystic Shrine. The bifocals bounced on the noses of the Sheiks-for-a-night and their ladies as the pearls of the Iowa desert bore them swiftly past the hot-dog stand, and everybody seemed to be having a good time. This is not true of the solemn military equitation groups that perform here, every man wondering what the C.O. will say to him if his horse breaks wind.

But to get back to our newspapers—

Harris, the antithesis of Kupcinet, is an in-print introvert. His column, on the *News* editorial page, is titled "Strictly Personal," and he often fills it with lists of "Purely Personal Prejudices," in the manner of H. L. Mencken's "Prejudices" in his *Smart Set* days. "Why doesn't some bright manufacturer put on the market a spiked platter from which a roast or a ham can't slip while it is being carved?" he wrote in a typical column not long ago. "All the clumsy-fingered carvers like myself would give him eternal thanks." But he is no mere clown. In the same column, he showed himself to be profound ("The greatest enemy of progress is the fanatical reformer—because he makes the world believe that all reformers are fanatics"), instructive ("No commonly-used word is so frequently mispronounced as 'irreparable' which should be accented on the second syllable"), esoteric ("The new summer styles for women boldly illustrate the truth of Lin Yutang's remark that 'all women's dresses, in every age and country, are merely variations on the eternal struggle between the admitted desire to dress and the unadmitted desire to undress' "), aesthetic ("One of the most passionate and defiant pieces of chamber music is the Schubert string quartet No. 15, as played on the new LP recording by the Vienna Konzerthaus Quartet. It's more shaking than a symphony"), and iconoclastic (" 'Oklahoma!' is perhaps the most overrated of all American musical plays; 'Dark of the Moon,' while not one-hundredth so successful, was far superior in almost every way"). Harris gives you a lot to think about. In any gathering of bright young Chicagoans, you are likely to find yourself arguing with Sydney Harris all over the place, even though he isn't there in person. And at any cocktail party to which you, as an out-of-towner, are invited to meet writers, you are almost sure to find him in person.

These cocktail parties, after I had been to several, began to remind me of a time in the spring of 1944 when a whole swarm of American war correspondents, including me, were spirited out of London by the Army and dropped at a place called Fowey, in Cornwall, where we were left on the hands of the commanding officer of a base for naval landing craft. The purpose of this excursion was to deceive any German spies who might be watching the war correspondents. The spies, seeing us disappear, would theoretically notify their bosses that the invasion was on. When we came back from Fowey, they would feel silly. The plan, I suppose, was for us to wear them out by a succession of such false alarms, but the real invasion started before we could complete the project. The C.O. at Fowey, who liked parties, caused it to be represented to the county families of the region that we were influential journalists who, for the sake of promoting international amity, should be entertained in their baronial keeps. The families were decent about it, but caused it to be represented to him that they had neither whiskey nor rations for hospitality. Accordingly, one afternoon, at the first baronial keep we were suffered to enter, the chatelaine, a blonde, steered us to an ancestral board presided over by a colored Navy messman in a white jacket, impersonating a feudal retainer. The board was laid out with ham sandwiches and the least expensive grade of Schenley's whiskey. We were then led out to the moat to have our pictures taken by a Navy photographer, and by the time we had said goodbye to the chatelaine and got over to the next keep, the same messman was all set up with some more ham sandwiches and a fresh supply of Schenley's. He must have raced ahead of us in a jeep. After our fourth keep, a correspondent with a vast appetite for Schenley's asked me if I didn't think it was funny all these county families having colored butlers. "And be damned," he said, sitting down in a bed of ancestral nettles, "if I don't think they all look the same."

At every party my wife and I went to in Chicago, we met Nelson Algren, whose novel "The Man with the Golden Arm" had just been published and well re-

viewed. Algren, who had never before had a popular
success, had stuck by his West Side Poles after all the
rest of the stark Chicago realists had fled to Hollywood, and he was still wearing steel-rimmed spectacles
and a turtle-neck sweater. He made no attempt to look
grim, however, and a diet of turkey, Virginia ham,
and cocktail shrimp apparently agreed with him; I
don't believe that for months he had an opportunity
to eat anything else. We were always glad to be introduced to each other, and even went out in private
a couple of times between parties. A man named
Milton Mayer, who writes articles for magazines, was
another standard act. The rest of the party was usually made up of admiring patrons of the arts and members of the faculty of the University of Chicago. For
a city where, I am credibly informed, you couldn't
throw an egg in 1925 without braining a great poet,
Chicago is hard up for writers.

The Chicago baseball teams of the National and
American Leagues have long languished, ignored,
in the second divisions of their organizations. Chicago
sports pages and taxi-drivers alike denounce them, but

without hope. Here is no spirit like Brooklyn's, peren-
nially reviviscent through disastrous years and rising
to ecstasy every time the Dodgers take both halves of a
doubleheader. Even last spring, sports-writers tell me,
when the White Sox had a long winning streak and
took the American League lead, the suspicious crowds
were slow to repair to the ball-park.[6] The fans don't
want to believe in their teams. It's the same in boxing;
no Chicago fighter has been a big Chicago drawing
card since Tony Zale, who emerged in the middle
thirties. (Zale was "out of" Gary, Indiana, but Gary is
one of the series of industrial suburbs that blend im-
perceptibly into the larger city.) In much smaller

[6] This was the occasion of a rebuke from a friend:

> Where did you ever get the idea that this town
> was not excited about the White Sox? You must have
> talked to some particularly weary sports-reporter by
> the name of Legion. I have never seen the damned
> town so excited over anything. I was offered twenty-
> five dollars a pair during the early summer for upper-
> deck box seats. When the Sox were leading the League,
> crowds gathered early around LaSalle Street news-
> stands listening to the vendor's radio. The Sox became
> temporarily a symbol of revived faith.

I shall not reveal his name, because he added, "Your
general thesis, however, is better than okay."

cities, like Youngstown, Hartford, or Providence—or, for that matter, in New York—a fighter has only to win a few bouts to get a neighborhood following, and a few more to be a town hero. Chicago skepticism about home talent is, in my estimation, a sign not of maturity but of a premature old age.

It is true that the *Tribune,* by devoting a preponderance of sports-page space to the huge annual amateur-boxing tournament called the Golden Gloves, a newspaper-promotion device, has helped put the professional game in the shade. Yet amateur boxing itself arouses no enthusiasm in Chicago. The *Tribune* now has to import boxers from places as remote as Memphis and Los Angeles for its "regional" championships. In the last of these championships that I witnessed, only one Chicagoan reached even the semifinal round.

Chicago is not particularly blessed with good restaurants. Byfield, its most energetic restaurateur until his death in 1950, used to say with pride that he was an engineer by training and a showman by inclination. He would invent dishes primarily for their spectacular possibilities—crabmeat wrapped in bacon and served flaming on a skewer, for example, or a salad of hearts of palm, Chinese water chestnuts, capers, bananas, and a highly spiced sauce. The first four ingredients of the salad cancel one another out, and the sauce makes the whole thing taste like the barbecued sandwiches the customers really like. "They won't come out to eat," Byfield told me sadly, a fortnight before his death. "They can eat at home. To get them out, you have to give them a show." Curiously, however, his fellow-citizens would come out for a show only if it was billed as a dinner. They would not patronize the shows he put on at his College Inn night club and billed as shows; a Chicagoan knows enough not to believe anything he sees in print. Byfield's restaurants became so theatrical they obliged him to abandon show business.

To compensate for the paucity of good restaurants, there are thousands of barbecues—usually spelled "Bar-B-cues"—that sell pig ribs roasted on a spit over a gas fire. These are appetizing, but always the same, and the natives eat them smothered with a hot sauce. To compensate for the lack of ordinary theatre, there are scores of strip-tease joints. The performances, like the pig ribs, are always the same, but they are invariably unpleasant. The most common form of strip joint is a long, narrow barroom with a rectangular or oval bar running up the middle; the girls work on a platform in the center, almost, but not quite, within the patrons' reach. The regular customers sit glumly on stools around the bar, trying to make a bottle of beer—priced at fifty cents—last all night. They must not concentrate too attentively on the girls, though, because the bartender sometimes tries to snatch the bottle while it is still a quarter full. The customer then has to buy another to retain his franchise. A master or a mistress of ceremonies introduces the girls and, in the course of his remarks, listlessly insults a stooge in the audience. ("Why don't you borrow two dollars and go out and get rid of them pimples?" the m.c. may ask a youthful gawk.) One of the girls, introduced as "Mlle. Yvonne Le Vonne, straight from Paris—and I mean Paris, Illinois, ha, ha," then goes through the familiar business of removing most of her specially constructed clothes, which have none of the sexual quality of other clothes. She does this with idiot gravity, and as a climax puts one foot on each side of the microphone shaft and does several kneebends. She then shakes herself as if she had just sat down on a spilled beer, and ends up by posing on one foot, with the other leg bent behind her. After that, she comes down into the crowd to cadge a drink, but she will settle for a cigarette if only the regular customers are present. Why they are present, night after night, is their own pathologically mysterious business. They are sad types, either adolescent or middle-aged, and though they are willing to pay a high price for the beer they drink, they are shabbier and of a more discouraged appearance than the clientele of other saloons.

The remunerative targets for the girls are the unknown drunks, wanderers from respectability, who come into the places in pairs or parties. Every joint has a permanent window sign reading, "Welcome, Conventioneers." No particular convention is specified; there are nearly a hundred of them a month in Chicago, and the joints are one of the principal, if usually unwritten, arguments in the selling of the city to convention secretaries. The girls attach themselves to the visiting drunks like tugboats to an incoming liner. They hustle them for drinks, and insult them if they're shunted off. But generally the drunks buy. After all, that's what they're there for. A girl granted the privilege of ordering a drink will have three in one—a shot glass of rye, a second of sweet vermouth, and a third of Coca-Cola. This retails for a dollar and thirty cents, or whatever multiple of it the bartender thinks fit to ask; he may set up a claim that the drunk has authorized drinks for two, three, or four girls besides the drink for the girl who has engaged him in conversation. The girls do not drink "downs"—soft drinks represented to the customers as whiskey. They apparently feel a need to stay as drunk as they can get without paying for it.

Two atypical conventioneers, one from North Hollywood, California, and the other from Old Greenwich, Connecticut, gave the newspapers ground for a good deal of fun a couple of years ago. It began on the night of April 19, 1950, when they declined to pay $28.35 for what they claimed were only eight drinks at a place called the French Casino, on North Clark Street. They finally paid, under what they interpreted as duress, but lest their indiscipline affect the behavior of future conventioneers, parties who eventually turned out to be unknown set upon them on the sidewalk outside and beat them senseless with small baseball bats. The conventioneers were under the impression these parties included the proprietor and his assistants. The use of small bats, in order not to kill the fellows, was an example of moderation, but they both proved unworthy of it. When they recovered consciousness, they crawled to a taxicab and asked to be taken to a police station. There was one practically right around the corner, on Chicago Avenue, but the driver, with fine presence of mind, drove them to a station a couple of miles away, where the lieutenant in command informed them he had no jurisdiction over North Clark Street. They had not specified *what* police station, the driver probably explained to them as he collected a fare of several dollars.

The unsporting pair persisted, and next morning they brought about the arrest of the proprietor of the Casino and the rest of the batting order as they remembered it. The police, perhaps stimulated by the Chicago Convention Bureau, which is opposed to local slaughter, at least before the guests have checked out, suspended the license of the establishment (its owner was reported in the newspapers to have an interest in three other places in the same police district, which were not affected), and the whole softball team, or at least the conventioneers' version of the lineup, was charged with felonious assault.

The case was set for hearing, and the battered guests stayed on to testify. But defense attorneys objected to the judge who was to preside at the trial and applied for a change of venue. A new judge was named, and on May 9th granted a continuance until May 22nd. The complainants thereupon went home, promising to return on the new date, which, undoubtedly to the defendants' astonishment, they did. The judge then granted another postponement, until June 27th, and the plaintiffs again went home, and again came back. It took three days to select a jury, and by that time the batting-practice targets, deciding it looked like all summer in Chicago for them if they stuck it out, had had enough. They went home for good. Municipal Judge Oscar S. Caplan, the presiding jurist, dismissed the jury, with sympathetic indignation. "It's a travesty on justice to waste your time and mine," he told the jurors, apparently not considering the time spent by the plaintiffs wasted, since travel is always instructive. The then Police Commissioner, John Prendergast, was more emphatic. "They are just out-of-towners who come in here and raise a lot of hell," he said to reporters. "They only raise hell to see what they can get out of it. We go ahead and do our part, and they fall flat on their faces." The captain of the Chicago Avenue police station had declared, upon first hearing of the case, that there were no clip joints in his satrapy, and that the battered men had probably been slugging each other. The effect of the affair upon the consuming public was excellent from the point of view of the North Clark Street strip-and-clip proprietors. Subsequent customers, knowing the penalty for adding up a check, have thought twice before being so vulgar.[7]

The Clark Street batting bee had an unfortunate

----

[7] Recalcitrance has reared its ugly head again, according to the following story from the *Sun-Times* of January 19, 1952.

social effect on my wife and me. A couple of days after it took place, a French friend, a member of the cultural service of the Embassy, visited Chicago to address a convention of language teachers, and came to

Chicago Briefs
CONVENTIONER'S BUDDY SIGNED,
TAVERN RAIDED

A conventioner from Fairfield, Conn., drew a map Friday to show police where his companion was singed in a brush against Chicago night life.

Gail C. Smith, 31, said he was struck by the "push button" entrance to the place when he visited it the other night with William H. Arnold, 31, of New York.

A press of a hidden button, he said, opened a steel door to a night club offering all the presumed conventioners' delights, including feminine companionship.

Smith said he left the place early and Arnold came back to their hotel later missing $125 in cash, a $100 check, a cigaret lighter and a wrist watch. Smith added that he diagnosed his companion's condition as a case of knockout drops.

With the aid of sketches Smith prepared of his taxi trip to the place, police found the button at the Coconut Isle Tavern, 3345 N. Western.

They pressed it and the door opened on a scene in which were six taxi drivers, five conventioners, five women and five employes of the place, including Lawrence Falco, 29, of 1025 Claremont, the manager.

All except the conventioners were arrested.

91

our house to dinner. Later in the evening, desiring to show him native culture, we escorted him to a strip-tease joint. We selected for this purpose a place of a slightly friendlier, as well as more pretentious, cast than the Casino, called the 606 Club, at 606 South Wabash Avenue. The 606 has a bar, but it is in the rear of the place, and there are tables between it and the blanket-size stage on which the girls perform. As evidence of character, there is a card on every table, reading:

Table No.   Waiter No.

$2.00 Minimum

Per Person

Food Included

Guest please check your table number with the waiter's check, any discrepancy please see Cashier or Floor Man.

It just shows that you go easy with some jerks and they creep all over you. Internal medicine is no good with a conventioneer. (I reject the *Sun-Times'* shortened spelling.) What them apes need is surgery.

The spaces after "Table No." and "Waiter No." on our card, however, were left blank.

The girls in the 606 appear a trifle better fed than those in the Clark Street places, and consequently exhibit a bit more spirit. On the evening we took our Frenchman, the first girl introduced walked onstage fully clothed. We smiled at our friend, and he smiled back with complicity; he had been told what was to come. He would be able to describe this strange rite to his friends in Paris when he next went home. The girl walked back across the stage, paused, and walked back without discarding so much as a glove. The conventioneers at the tables around us clapped to encourage her. She walked across again, still fully clothed, and for three minutes she just kept on walking. I have seldom seen a woman's face record such embarrassment. Remaining clothed was obviously as much of an ordeal for her as stripping in public would have been for a dowager. Our friend regarded us with an air *étonné;* the conventioneers looked gloomy. Six successive girls went through practically the same performance. One of them made a lamentable attempt at a tap dance; another, coaxed by the master of ceremonies, sang a couple of lines of a song and then broke into a nervous giggle.

"But it's very *moral*," our Frenchman said. "It is like the commencement exercise at a seminary for young ladies. I feel almost as if I were to present the prize for proficiency in Romance languages."

After finishing our two-dollar minimums, including no food (the only food that could possibly fit into the minimum, if you had one drink, would be a cherry, if the drink happened to be a Manhattan), we headed for the door. Remembering the boys' baseball bats, I hesitated to complain, but I timidly asked the man who guides you to your tables if the show wasn't somehow different from the way I remembered it.

"Sure," he said. "The lid's on."

A *Tribune* editorial cartoon, celebrating the award last May of the national Republican convention for 1952 to Chicago, showed "Chicago, the Convention Queen" as a female figure draped in long robes of virginal white. I hope it is not a forecast.

3.

The Massacree

··

T HE city of Chicago, on the west shore of Lake
Michigan, is less one town than a loose confederacy of
fifty wards. To bind them together, the wards have not
even climate, since the waters of the Lake retain
warmth on into the fall and intense cold through June,
with the result that there is sometimes a difference of a
much as twenty degrees in temperature between the
Lake shore and the interior. The inhabitants of the
city, therefore, cannot use the weather as a common

topic of conversation. The heart of the city, as small in proportion to its gross body as a circus fat lady's, succeeds in pumping most Chicagoans through it barely more than once a year, and then just to view the Christmas decorations set out by the department-store owners on State Street. The people in the majority of the wards, remote from this heart, work in the wards they live in—those living near the Stockyards, for example, work in the Stockyards, and those near Inland Steel at Inland. If a man has a job outside the ward he sleeps in, it is likely to be in one just as far from the center of town. In this, Chicago is the antithesis of Washington and New York, where there is a universal movement of the working inhabitants—toward the center of the city in the morning, centrifugal in the evening.

Communication between the residents of the different wards is further limited by the pronounced tendency of immigrant groups in Chicago to coagulate geographically. In Chicago, a man known as a Pole or a Norwegian may not have been born in Poland or Norway, or of parents born there. If even only his grandparents were so born, he refers to himself as a Pole or

a Norwegian if he wants to sell coffins or groceries or life insurance to others like himself. A national identification is absolutely essential if he wishes to enter politics. A Chicago party ticket is an international patchwork, like Europe after the Treaty of Versailles. Most of the members of the Chicago national blocs, however, think of Europe as it was cut up by the Congress of Vienna. The great waves of immigration that carried them or their forefathers to their jobs in this country ended with the beginning of the First World War, and they lack the sense of contact with Europe that is sustained by the coming and going of ships, as in New York. To Chicago Norwegians, Norway remains a backward peasant country—"with goats on the roof," as one social-service worker puts it. These Norwegians were isolationists during the war, while their Brooklyn compatriots, who were in a position to talk with Norwegian sailors, were interventionists. To Chicago Croats or Chicago Serbs, Yugoslavia is an unexperienced concept. Poland, to Chicago Poles, means Catholicism and street parades. Chicago has no liberal Italian-American political leaders, like La-Guardia, Poletti, or even Pecora; to be Italian in Chicago means to be loyal to the Italian political machine in the Italian wards. The Irish continue to boil over about the famine of 1846–47. The national blocs are as entirely cut off from Europe as they are from the rest of America—or from the next ward. And the division between the Negro wards and the white is even more drastic.

To make the wards breathe as one calls for an event like the Fire of 1871 or the Columbian Exposition of 1893. The Haymarket riot of 1886, when somebody or other threw a bomb that killed several policemen, and the Black Sox scandal of 1920, when the city learned that its American League team had sold the World Series of the previous year, were other happenings of the magnitude required. The wards are as jealous of their political sovereignty as Ulster or the Union of South Africa. The aldermen do not hesitate to snub the Mayor, a moving-and-storage man named Martin H. Kennelly, who looks like a bit player impersonating a benevolent banker. Kennelly, the aldermen are fond of saying (as if they had never heard of Samuel Insull), "must be honest, because he doesn't need the money," but when he tries to assert himself, they react as if they had been kicked by a stained-glass window.

I have been a visitor to Chicago several times in the past few years, but it was only during the winter of 1949-50, when my wife, my stepdaughter, and I were residents, that I had a chance to get to know the aldermen well. At that time, they gave an entrancing display of their free spirit by blocking a plan to provide low-cost housing for twelve thousand families, out of the two hundred thousand who, according to one reliable estimate, are in need of it. The federal government had earmarked the necessary funds for this purpose, and the Mayor had appointed a Chicago Housing Authority, which, after study, had approved sites for the buildings. But every site lay within some alderman's ward—a difficulty impossible to avoid, since all Chicago is divided into wards. Few aldermen wanted new housing within their own wards; it might loosen the landlords' grip on their established constituents. Even worse, it might bring an influx of new voters to upset the ward's political balance and the alderman himself.

An idea of how serious the subject of housing is in

Chicago may be gathered by this passage from a piece that Walter White, Executive Secretary of the National Association for the Advancement of Colored People, wrote for the New York *Herald Tribune* following the Cicero riots last summer:

As part of the background, let's look at the plight of Harvey Clark and his wife Johnetta, also a college graduate, and their two children, aged eight and six. The Clarks moved to Chicago from Nashville, Tenn., in 1949. At first he worked as an insurance salesman and later as a bus driver for the Chicago Transit Authority. Because as a Negro he was restricted in finding a home, the best accommodation he could secure was one-half of a small two-room apartment on Chicago's South Side, for which he paid $12.50 a week, or approximately $56 a month. The Clarks occupied a tiny bedroom while another family of five occupied the equally small living room. The apartment was located in a vermin-infested building which can most charitably be described as a firetrap.

Many of the white wards are almost as congested, and the spillover of Negroes from their intolerably crowded neighborhoods into the scarcely less jammed wards around them sets the stage for the racial violence that is Chicago's greatest present danger. Racial feeling is harsh; it isn't just a matter of the riots that get into the newspapers, but a continual edginess.

For example, I have seen a white couple, laden down with bundles after an afternoon's Christmas shopping, pass up a colored taxi-driver on State Street, though cabs were scarce. They apparently preferred to stand and shiver until they could get a white man. I got into the cab after they, to my amazement, had waved it on, and on the way home I asked the driver if I had rightly understood the little scene. He said I had. "They passed me up because I was colored," he said. "A lot of them do." [1]

Chicago crowding is still a crowding into one- or two-story, one- or two-family dwellings, as it was in

----

[1] I will concede the possibility that there are New Yorkers who will take a white driver in preference to a Negro when either is available; but I have never seen one who would freeze for his ill feelings.

1906, when Upton Sinclair brought out "The Jungle," describing the Lithuanian and Polish workers in the Stockyards. The slums look more like Hoovervilles than Harlems. In this horizontal crowding, the proprietors of all the tar-paper-and-matchwood buildings fear the economic threat of the multiple-family housing development.

One of the advantages of this type of housing, from a landlord's point of view, becomes evident in the following story from the Chicago *Daily News,* sometime last June:

Authorities Pass the Buck
QUERIES ON FIRETRAPS
GET REPORTER NOWHERE
BUILDING IN WHICH 3 DIED
UNSAFE, CORONER'S JURY RULES

Who is going to investigate the "unsafe and hazardous condition" of the 3-story building at 1736 N. Clark in which three elderly men lost their lives in a fire May 11?

A Daily News Reporter set out to find the answer to that question.

He got nowhere.

A coroner's jury ruled Wednesday that the three men—Thomas McGeeghan, 80; John Nordlund, 80, and Carl Laubengaier, 68—died accidentally in the fire in the house owned by Mrs. Anna Anbach, 69, who lived in the building.

The jury found also that the building was kept in an "unsafe and hazardous condition and recommended an investigation by "proper authorities."

But just who are the "proper authorities"?

The building had never been inspected by the city because buildings of that size are considered private residences if they have less than 10 tenants. This building had nine.[2]

....

[2] The story, as it chanced, ran on an inside page of the same issue of the *News* that contained Mr. Pettibone's paean, part of which I cited earlier. In another portion of his piece Mr. Pettibone listed some recent advances made in Chicago civic life.

Among them was: "Adoption of a modern building code and a start on enforcement of minimum housing standards through adequate inspection."

The 1700 block on North Clark, by the way, is not in

The aldermen, who constitute the City Council, rejected the Housing Authority's sites and turned the quest for new ones into a form of slapstick. At one point, they proposed to place all twelve thousand family units in the vicinity of the University of Chicago, far from the worst overcrowding. This was a broadly comic dig at Bob Merriam, the young alderman from the Fifth Ward, which includes the University. Merriam had been one of the few members of the Council to support the Housing Authority's sites. It was all good, clean fun, and the housing never got built, although the Council has since approved some sites, on three or four of which work may commence this spring. Meanwhile, the two hundred thousand families continue to live in sub-standard homes.

Merriam is a town character—an honest alderman. In any of the better residential neighborhoods, one meets him at practically every party one attends; it is typical of well-off Chicagoans to be passionately inter-

some outer Bronx or Newlots of Chicago, but spang in the middle of the city, no farther from the Loop than 75th Street is from Times Square.

ested in good government. Merriam is a lively man in his mid-thirties, who has inherited his taste for politics from his father. The elder Merriam, a professor emeritus of political science at the University, once ran for Mayor of Chicago on a reform ticket. In the son, the delighted observer frequently gets ahead of the idealist. "Chicago is unique," he said to me the first time I met him. "It is the only completely corrupt city in America." When I told him I had heard a couple of other places equally ill spoken of, he said defensively, "But they aren't nearly as big."

This ambivalence is a Chicago characteristic. People you meet at a party devote a great deal more time than people elsewhere to talking about good government, but they usually wind up the evening boasting about the high quality of the crooks they have met. At every social gathering, abuse is heaped upon the head of every politician in public view, the standard complaint being that the fellow is not sufficiently idealistic. The male guests carry five-dollar bills folded in their drivers' licenses. Upon being stopped by a traffic policeman, they present the license, the cop takes the fin and returns the license, and the transaction is closed. "He had me, all right," is the customary explanation. "Why should I bother to go to court to pay a fine?"

These same people are constantly in quest of intellectual improvement. "We'd like to invite you over to dinner tonight," one of our best Chicago friends told us on the telephone the second day we were in town, "but we've turned over our house for the evening to our Group for an informal discussion of the devaluation of the pound." Everybody you meet belongs to a Great Books Discussion Group; the study of the Great Books can last a lifetime, even when the samplings taken of them are exceedingly small. (Two chapters of Gibbon, thoroughly digested in a discussion group led by one's chiropodist, are supposed to be the equivalent of the whole work merely read.) In Chicago intellectual circles, a man who can't do a psychoanalysis between two Martinis ranks with a fellow who can't change a tire. A man condemned to earn his living by writing, and therefore accustomed to talk about football or the proper temperature of beer, finds himself conversationally impaled by determined ladies who want to discuss Lionel Trilling. Intellectual Chicagoans are all desperately earnest and seem as wholly isolated as the second-generation Croats. The wards stretch out around the lakeside apartment houses, or Gold Coast, and around the University and the pleasant detached houses near it, where the serious thinkers live, and the wards are unaffected by anything the people in those houses think or say.

Because there is very little low-priced housing, Chicagoans have set up a Housing Council, and because there is much crime, they have set up a Crime Commission, and because relations between whites and blacks are bad, a Commission on Human Relations, but everything remains very much the same, for these organizations operate in a vacuum. The conviction that anything in the world can be ameliorated by setting up a council or forming a committee is as much an article of faith with Chicagoans of good will as the notion that there is a short cut to every intellectual objective (except business success, which, of course, demands full-time thought in all waking hours not set aside specifically for culture). The city is not only the home of the short analysis and of the theory that a liberal culture can be acquired by reading arbitrarily chosen slivers of a number of arbitrarily chosen books; it also has the only large university that awards a liberal-arts degree for an undergraduate course that starts after the second year of high school and ends after what would anywhere else be the second year of college. As a result of this generous stand, the University of Chicago's undergraduate college acts as the greatest magnet for neurotic juveniles since the Children's Crusade, with Robert Maynard Hutchins, the institution's renovator, until recently playing the role of Stephen the Shepherd Boy in the revival. Walking inadvertently (I can't imagine anyone's doing it on purpose) into any of the campus taverns along Fifty-fifth Street, the University's equivalent of the Boulevard St. Michel, the adult stranger finds himself in a kind of juvenile Alsatia, where the male voices haven't changed yet. By conversation with the inmates, he may learn, as I did from one lad, that "the strong point about Chicago is it's the only university where you can hold a full-time daytime job and still get your B.A. You don't have to go to class at all. Just read the Great Books and work up a line for the comprehensive examination at the end of the year." There is no general public institution of higher learning in Chicago, and the opportunity to work full time is often necessary to the earning of tuition fees. But a B.A. is a B.A., and if Dr. Lawrence A. Kimpton, who not long ago succeeded Hutchins as chancellor of the University, decides to accept candidates out of the third grade instead of the tenth, he will probably be hailed on the Midway as an even greater educational innovator.

[*Academic Amplification*

[A doctor in Urbana, Ill., wrote to me that talking to the undergraduates about a college was as vain as trying to learn about an army from the enlisted men, or, as he put it, EMs. I am in favor of both procedures.

[A learned office boy at *The New Yorker* (B.A.

University of Chicago, 1950) has contributed the following amplification:

The real truth is that, in the College—and not the "Divisions" (junior year of regular college and up), *no* papers are required. The mark in the course is determined entirely by a six-hour objective exam, which is give at the end of the year. This is called a "Comprehensive" ("comp" for short) and consists of complete-the-statement-correctly questions, and sometimes there is a short essay question, the subject of which is never given out in advance. On the English composition exam, two essays are assigned—their subject is not known until the student is in the examination room. Sometimes, however, the Board of Examination cannot resist the scientific instinct and gives a short section of objective questions on English style. This section, like all objective sections—is marked by an IBM machine, which is apparently the newest thing in education since the Great Books. (Incidentally this gives rise to a strange academic occupation. During examination periods, the Board of Examinations finds it necessary to hire a girl for eight hours a day for the sole purpose of sharpening the special pencils needed to make out the IBM answer sheets, which are graded electrically.) To get back to papers, none, even in English composition, are compulsory except those on the comps.

This system of comprehensive exams usually makes the student say—when describing the system to his friends and relatives back home—"All you gotta do is pay the fees and pass the comp." Reading books, writing papers, studying, are overshadowed by the comp.

[From a graduate student of Government now at an Eastern university, who spent last year in Chicago:

I went to the U. of C. with the suspicion that Laski had been harsh in his cracks about Hutchins and the neo-Thomists looking to the Middle Ages to forget the slums, stockyards and gangsters on the South Side. He wasn't.

[I had a reproving note from a Harvard faculty wife who, she said, was Chicago-born. It ended:

P.S. As I think back it is *how* you have said a lot of things—not always what you have said. I find myself a critic of Hutchins, and I thought the students I knew at the University of Chicago dull socially and Neurotic—and—and—and I was sick when I thought my husband might take a job there,—and I'd half to live around there. ["Half" for "have" from an educated woman, is a revealing slip; she may have felt that she would be only half alive if compelled to inhabit her home town.] But the way you said it made me want to defend the whole kit and kaboodle of them. And I don't like them at all.

[The bearer of one of the premium names in the meat-packing industry, who describes himself in his letter as "a graduate of the University of Chicago, and expatriate who has no desire to go back," writes in part:

One of my pet theories is that the flatness of the region is largely responsible for the city as it is.—The spreading flatness made possible those wooden slums and the dreary houses and apartment buildings of the ordinary folks. Indeed the curiously futile darts of many Chicago people up towards culture may be partly due to their flat foundation.—Hutchins and the Hundred Books are like attempts at synthetic books and mountains.

[No portion of my *New Yorker* series provoked more hot written words than my brief allusion to this intellectual foundling asylum, the undergraduate college of the University, whose inmates I viewed with sympathy, like the Little Princes in the Tower, or Hänsel and Gretel in the cage.

[The graduate faculties, which resisted *Gleichschaltung* with open rebellion against the impresario some years ago, are still on a pinnacle of prestige, especially in the natural sciences, about which I am not qualified to have an opinion.

[This reminds me of a French restaurant-owner I knew in Paris during the static *drôle de guerre*. He took a dim view of the British, who as yet had sent no troops into the line. But even he approved of the headlines telling about the sinking of the *Graf von Spee*, the German pocket battleship, by two British cruisers. "It appears they are superb," he said, "but not where I can see them!"]

A superb specimen of a Chicago alderman is Paddy Bauler, who represents the Forty-third Ward. Bauler's De Luxe Gardens, at North Avenue and Sedgwick, is as sedate a groggery as you will come upon in the city of Chicago. It occupies the former premises of the Immigrant State Bank, which went under in the crash, and the original lavatory solemnity of the interior's marble décor has never been altered. The high ceilings, the grilles barring the way to the vaults, and all the other accessories designed to nurture unfounded confidence remain to warn of the uncertainty of appearances, and the patrons conduct themselves as discreetly as men about to solicit a loan. It is here that the Alderman, who is also a member of the Cook County Democratic Committee, holds court, like Saint

Louis of France under his tree of judgment, from nine to eleven each evening, when he is not travelling in Europe. Paddy travels often, and always in style; he says that trips to places like Rome and Palestine help him to understand the different kinds of people in his ward. The saloon's license is in his brother's name. Paddy has apparently done well at making his aldermanic salary of five thousand dollars a year stretch.

The Alderman is a mountain—or, rather, since his contours are soft, a gravel dump—of a man, with a wide pink face wearing an expression of mock truculence. Twenty years ago, when he was courting the attention of Mayor Tony Cermak, he used to roll about the floor in wrestling matches with himself to make His Honor laugh; he weighed two hundred and seventy-five pounds then, and he has put on several ounces since. He is essentially decorous, however; a few nights before Christmas of 1933 he shot a policeman who wanted him to serve a drink after hours. Paddy had locked up and was depositing the receipts from a Forty-third Ward Democratic Christmas Fund benefit show in the bank vault when the policeman came to the door raucously demanding admittance.

Paddy went out to quiet him. "Johnny, why have I got this coming to me for?" the Alderman roared plaintively. "I never done anything to you." Then he shot the policeman, and nobody has used bad language or tried to get a drink after hours in the De Luxe Gardens since. Only a few years ago, a man named Kane, who was opposing Paddy in the Democratic primary in the ward, complained because the store he was using for his headquarters was bombed one night. Kane claimed to be a close friend of Mayor Kennelly's. The Alderman said things were coming to a pretty pass when a fellow would bomb his own headquarters for publicity. "I wouldn't have minded it so much," he told reporters, "if the guy hadn't run up there and stuck Kennelly's picture in the broken window before the cops came." Paddy's posters in a recent election campaign said, with elegant restraint, "Elect Mathias J. Bauler. He will appreciate your vote." Paddy doesn't have to make himself known to the voters in the Forty-third. Once, he says, he told a campaign audience that he had been the first child ever christened in St. Teresa's Church, in his ward. The pastor looked up the baptismal record and, sure enough, Paddy had been.

Paddy's father was born in Germany, and his mother in Illinois, of German descent. Like many other men of non-Irish descent who spend their lives in politics, he has acquired a Celtic manner that sometimes imposes on him, just as some non-Frenchmen who work their way up in the restaurant business begin to think of themselves as French. Paddy's ward, it happens, is so ethnologically scrambled that there is no great political profit in being any particular kind of European, but among politicians the rule is: When in doubt, be Irish. "I've almost forgotten my name is Mathias," Paddy says.

There is no entertainment—not even a dice girl— in the De Luxe Gardens. North Avenue, which begins near Lake Michigan and runs straight west through the dimness until it hits the city line, lies only a little over a mile and a half north of the Loop, but it is the axis of an autonomous dreariness. The eastern end of the avenue, which is in Paddy's ward, has a small night life, with a German-language movie house, one or two German restaurants with zither players, and some Hungarian saloons, through which wander, in the course of the evening, a few fiddlers, who say that they are gypsies but that they have forgotten the Old Country music, because they are never asked for it. The favorite request numbers of Chicago Hungarians are "Tennessee Waltz" and "When Irish Eyes Are Smiling." Also, there are numerous bars that use low prices as their chief sales argument. These places seem purposely bare and flimsy, as if to assure the customers that nothing is being wasted on overhead. The liquor-license fee is low in Chicago, and the sheer number of saloons, even in backwash neighborhoods, is amazing. Curbstones are high, often consisting of two steps instead of one, and drunks sometimes take astonishing falls. These are seldom fatal. "You're like all us Polacks," I once heard a North Avenue bartender say to a patron who had had all he could drink. "One ain't enough and a thousand ain't enough." Then the patron went out and crashed on his head. "You can't kill a Polack," the bartender said.

The Forty-third Ward is one of the most diversified in the city, containing in its lakeward corner half of the Gold Coast, including the two Ambassador Hotels, the Cardinal's Residence, and Colonel Robert R. McCormick's town house. Toward the ward's south-west frontier there is a Negro slum (not the great one but an isolated growth), in its center is the residue of the original German colony, and within its boundaries are also blocs of Nisei, Finns, Hungarians, Italians, Irish, Syrians, Armenians, Swedes, and Poles, and a couple of neighborhoods of flats and one-family residences inhabited by solid settlers of the middle class from Iowa and Nebraska. Parts of the ward look like a city, parts like a pleasant suburb, and large tracts like the less favored sections of a blighted mill town. The principle of Paddy's rule is simple. "Everybody gets something," he says.

During one of my longer stays in Chicago I lived in the Forty-third, and I ran across a friend of mine —and a constituent of Paddy's—who volunteered to take me over to the De Luxe Gardens to meet the gentleman. The friend, a fellow named Martin, was brought up in the ward, where his father, a carpenter and novelist born in Finland, owned a house. Martin started out to be a novelist, too, but somehow landed in the advertising business, which keeps him prosperous and embarrassed. He is a victim of his present environment, in which literature no longer flourishes; if he had been born ten years earlier in Chicago, I am convinced, he would have been a novelist, proud and famishing. We found Paddy sitting at a table with one of his executive assistants, a younger man, who also owns a saloon and is training to be an officeholder. "I am always here at nine o'clock, in case anybody has a brother that has been arrested or a relative he wants to get into Cook County Hospital or anything like that," the Alderman said. "I am A-1 with the Hospital," he went on, and explained that without support, a candidate for admission has to wait his turn. "You got to keep in touch," he said. "Things like that the precinct captain should be on the lookout for, if they are in his precinct, but you can't always depend on them."

Paddy told me that there were forty thousand votes in his ward, and that in his capacity as Democratic Committeeman he had seventy-six precinct captains, each with a city, state, or county job. "We have some very nice jobs to give out, from two hundred and seventy up to three hundred and fifty dollars a month," he said. "And all the fellow has to do is keep track of the votes in his precinct and get out the Democratic voters when it counts. If he says there will be one hundred votes for us and eighty for the other fellow, I would rather have it come out that way than one hundred and fifty to twenty, because if it comes out the second way, it shows the precinct captain don't know his business, or he is faking. I got to know within one per cent. That's how I know if I got good precinct captains. Then I got to tell the county chairman how the vote will be in the ward. That's how he knows if he's got a good committeeman. Naturally, if I got a bum precinct captain, I got to get rid of him and give that city job to a hustler, because if I got enough bum captains, it will throw my figures out. Then I am a bum, too."

"And have you always been able to tell what the vote in the ward will be?" I asked.

"I never been off the public payroll in forty years," the Alderman replied, with modest indirection. "The second big thing a precinct captain has to do is get out the vote. The way he does that is by knowing everybody in his precinct and being nice to them. Everybody needs a favor sometimes, but some people are too dumb to ask for it. So I say to my captains, 'If you notice a hole in the sidewalk in front of a fellow's house, call on him a week before election and ask him if he would like it fixed. It could never do any harm to find out.' When you got a good precinct captain, you got a jewel. Like last year. It was an off year and hard to get people interested, but we needed some votes to elect local candidates. I asked a young fellow named Barney McGuirl how many votes he thought he'd get out in his precinct and he said about ninety-five. 'Well,' I said, 'Barney, I know you got five beautiful little children and a bailiff's salary does not go as far as it should,' I said, 'although I hope to get you something a little better soon. But if you get me a hundred and fifty votes just this time, I will present them angels with ten dollars apiece.' He got me a hundred and ninety-seven.

"We got nice people in this ward," Paddy went on. "Nice Germans, nice Poles, nice Irish, nice Jews, nice colored people, and so on, and recently we been getting a lot of Japanese, which are moving north across Division Street, and they are a very nice high-class class of Japanese. I try to see that nobody gets shut out on the jobs. The Forty-third Ward, I always say when I make a speech, is like the United Nations."

The Gold Coast, although it confers social éclat on the ward, is not Paddy's favorite corner. "The type people you got over there don't need a job as bailiff, so you got to rely on amateurs for your organization work," he said. Moreover, he holds that the inhabitants of the Gold Coast, many of whom are Republicans, expect more than their share of service. "They complain about dirty streets and bad lighting and fads like that, and about they never got enough cops, and when you come right down to it, they got only one vote apiece, like everybody else," he told me. "But it's a fine ward. We had the Massacree in this ward. Did you know that?"

"The what?" I asked.

The effect of my failure to comprehend was unfortunate. *"The St. Valentine's Massacree,* of course!" Paddy shouted. Then, regaining control of himself, he added, "Right over in a garage in the 2100 block on Clark. I knew some of the fellows." The Alderman's manner, if not his tone, was that of Dr. Douglas Southall Freeman saying, "There stood Pickett's men."

I was impressed. I had, naturally, heard about the St. Valentine's Day Massacre of 1929, in which some gangsters line up seven competitors against a wall and slaughtered them, and I was familiar with the 2100 block on Clark, for it was just around the corner from the Francis W. Parker School, which my stepdaughter was attending, but I had not been aware that there was any connection between the two or that I had frequently walked past a shrine.

"Were the fellows you knew shot?" I asked the Alderman. "Or did they do the shooting?"

"They were shot," he said, giving me my first intimation that the home team had lost.

"The Gusenbergs weren't bad kids," Paddy said. "Just wild. They were working for a bootlegger, that's all." Now he sounded like a man who had known General Custer. Frank Gusenberg, a boy from the ward, had been the hero of the Massacree, although I didn't know it then. I have since learned that Frank, left for dead among the corpses, was found still breathing and was transported to the Alexian Brothers' Hospital, where he survived for an hour, and then died "true to gangland's immemorial code," as one newspaper put it, refusing to say who had shot him. Local historians resolutely reject the hypothesis that he didn't know. Someday he undoubtedly will have his statue.

I tried my story of Paddy Bauler and the Massacree on a non-practicing lady novelist, sixtyish, of distinguished Chicago lineage and social position, who once won a Pulitzer Prize and is on most subjects a well-balanced woman. With gay excitement, she cried, "How I remember that afternoon! I went around to Francis Parker to call for my daughter. But all the children had cut classes and gone to view the scene! Those were wonderful times!" A matron who, as a young newspaperwoman, did a feature story on the bloodstained garage spoke of the day with the same nostalgia. I could well believe that since then life for her had been an anticlimax.

Feeling that I was for the first time on the verge of discovering something that would help me understand Chicago, I hurried to the morgue of the *Sun-Times* to enrich my recollection of the local epopee. The Massacree had occurred, I read, in a garage at 2122 North Clark Street. Seven men—six thugs and an optometrist who was, like many Chicagoans of his day, a crime buff with a penchant for impressing his friends by dropping names—had been lounging around some trucks in the garage on the morning of the 14th when, at about ten o'clock, an automobile drove up to the curb and four men got out. Two of the men from the automobile were wearing police uniforms and carrying submachine guns and the other two were in ordinary clothes and were armed with sawed-off shotguns. The four men entered the garage. After about half an hour, they came out, first the pair in ordinary clothes, who were now unarmed and walked with their hands over their heads, as if prisoners. The two in police uniforms were right behind them, and kept their guns pointed at their backs. A Mrs. Alphonsine Morin, street-watching from a window of No. 2125, across the way, had seen it all. North Clark must have been an interesting street to live on at that time, for she didn't think the scene unusual enough to call to her neighbors' attention. Presently, somebody walked into the garage and found Frank Gusenberg wallowing in his blood, and the corpses of six men, including Dr. Reinhardt H. Schwimmer, the name-dropper.

The way the victims had fallen indicated that they had been lined up facing a wall, as if to submit to a search for arms. Noting this, and hearing about the men in police uniforms, the first reporters on the scene decided that the Forty-third Warders had been betrayed by their confidence in the Chicago police. The victims, so the reasoning went, had assumed they were going to be taken to a station house for a shakedown, which wasn't worth fighting over, and had therefore not resorted to their own weapons. The police, in denying this theory, were highly indignant about the executioners' ruse, evidently fearing no gangsters would ever trust them again. The next morning's papers reported all the town's speakeasies closed, "criminals missing from their usual haunts," and "a relentless investigation unclenched." (Who, I have often wondered, clenches an investigation?) Arthur Sears Henning, the Chicago *Tribune's* chief Washington correspondent, viewing the event from the capital, blamed "alien gangs that have been terrorizing Chicago."

Crime reporters wrote like Lippmanns and Alsops in those days, and one of these seers of the bigger picture asserted that the North Side gang had been stricken by its "historic antagonist, as history goes in the swift careers of gangsters"—the South Side gang. It was, almost all the reporters agreed, a tragic chapter in the bloody story of the North Side Dynasty of Dion O'Banion, Hymie Weiss, Schemer Drucci, and Bugs Moran, who had already been done in or had disappeared and who, in long biographical résumés, were pictured as victims of their own chivalry. Their opponents, the Colosimo-Torrio-Capone Dynasty, were deprecated as consistently unethical. Their latest demonstration of this quality, the writers predicted, might well affect the balance of power in International Gangdom. Meanwhile, a lady reporter wrote that she had watched detectives strip large diamond rings from the stiffening fingers of the victims, proving that not robbery but revenge had been the motive. It also proved that the killers had not been bona-fide detectives, who would have got the rings in the first place for sure.

It was my impression that nobody had ever been punished for taking part in the Massacree. I found, consulting the *Sun-Times'* clippings, that this was correct. The police eventually decided they knew who the shooters were, but by the time they had made up their minds, all the putative marksmen had themselves been massacreed, except a man by the name of Burke, who was then at large and later wound up in prison for killing a police officer in St. Joseph, Michigan. Burke died in stir in 1940—true, the press noted, to gangland's immemorial code.

In the *Sun-Times'* morgue, I came across some very beautiful retrospective pieces about the Massacree, most of them written on anniversaries of the event. One, by a man named Larry Kelly, in the *Sun* of February 14, 1943, began, "St. Valentine's Day in Chicago doesn't always call up thoughts of heart-shaped boxes and pretty verses. Forever linked with that day is the memory of that morning of February 14, 14 years ago. . . ." The tenderest, I thought, was by a fellow named Clem Lane, of the Chicago *Daily News.* "There had been snow flurries that morning as the mailmen made their rounds, their loads made heavier by the lovers' missives," he wrote, also in 1943. Further on, his style hardened: "There was talk of a reward of $100,000 for the apprehension of the kill-

ers. The City Council voted $20,000 for such a re-
ward, but spent it on something else when the heat
died down." There was no lack of fresher shooting to
write about in 1943, I reflected, and thousands of Chicagoans were abroad in the thick of it. But the spell of
the Massacree persisted. It was Chicago's own.

When I felt myself sufficiently documented, I made
a pilgrimage by taxi to 2122. There is not even a
modest historical plaque on the exterior of the building, which has been converted into a warehouse. The
driver, to whom I explained the purpose of my trip,
was much impressed. "I've heard Al Capone was a
good guy," he said. "He run soup kitchens during the
depression."

There have been gang homicides in Chicago since
the Massacree—at least a hundred and eighty-eight
since 1932, according to an estimate published in
1950. Public interest, however, has flagged. On Sep-
tember 25, 1950, for example, a former Chicago police lieutenant, William J. Drury, who had been acting
as a tipster for the Kefeuvar Committee in Chicago,
was shot to death as he sat in his car in the garage be-

hind his home. The story had attractive features: Drury was said to have owned "a little black notebook" with all the dope about Chicago crime in it, he had received threatening telephone calls, and he had got in touch with the Kefauver people a few hours before his death to say he needed protection. Chicago didn't rise to the bait. "The police investigation followed the routine pattern in gang killings," the *Tribune* reported, two days after the crime. "The inquest into Drury's death was continued after his widow testified she knew of no reason why anyone should want to kill her husband. All law enforcement authorities pledged co-operation in the man hunt. No one was arrested." In due course it was reported, "The investigation of the shotgun slaying of former police lieutenant William Drury [seems] to be fading out," and on November 28th the coroner declared the inquest formally closed. I missed the fine frenzy of the old Massacree stories, with their talk of dynasties and immemorial codes. Nowadays, nobody in Chicago even mentions the Drury murder.

The city's tendency to live in the past since the Massacree—as shown by its muted reaction to the Drury case, which in the twenties would have been considered a creditable murder—is a peculiar one. I have tried to account for it by the hypothesis that the Massacree, like the Dionne quintuplets, set too high a standard of performance for the maintenance of public interest in the future. Just as no multiple birth short of six will ever again seem newsworthy, so the Chicago gangster ambitious to make an impression is confronted with the task of killing at least *eight* people at a clip, preferably including a minimum of *two* professional men —perhaps a chiropractor and a podiatrist—and preferably on Mother's Day or Christmas Eve. (The Fourth of July, by the way, also offers tempting possibilities for a massacree. I know a man in Rhode Island whose father used to go out and shoot a deer every time the date came around, on the safe assumption that the game warden would think the shot part of the celebration.)

The hold the Massacree has on the civic memory is not entirely dependent on the number of casualties. A couple of years ago, a streetcar collided with a gasoline trailer tank truck and thirty-two passengers were burned to death, but the event shows no signs of entering into legend. Nor has it had any effect on the life of the community. The streetcars still run at the same insane speed and the trailers are of the same unwieldy length as before; Chicagoans view such hazards with equanimity, like the railroad crossings at grade that intersect their principal streets. The gasoline companies deserve the same consideration as the railroads, sensible Chicagoans say; after all, nobody contests the Stockyards' right to smell. The *Tribune* no longer bothers to print its editorial "Program for Chicagoland," which included, as Points 4 and 5, "Abolish the Smoke Pall" and "Grade Separation on Thru Streets and Boulevards." The smoke pall is the town's concession to the steel plants. As Paddy says, "Everybody gets something."

The Massacree has held Chicago's interest partly because the gangster years coincided with those of the Great Bubble. That was when Insull built his pyramids of holding companies, Cutten and other heroes slaughtered invaders in the grain market, and the world looked as promising as a pool table with

a hanger on every pocket. All that ended soon after
the Massacree. Primarily, the Massacree focussed attention on the town. I have known Chicagoans who
claim that they are embarrassed, when they are travelling abroad, at being quizzed about *les gangsters.* I
have never believed them, because they invariably tell
it like a funny story. They remind me of a movie star
telling what a bore it is to be recognized. As for the
kids in the drearinesses of the wards, they have always
loved Chicago's reputation. Citizens of a city celebrated in the movies, they are little Scarfaces as they
sit with their molls in the darkened cinemas and iden-
tify themselves with the glorious past.

The great tradition has left its mark. Only the real
gangsters and their molls no longer dress like gangsters and their molls, if the witnesses before the Kefauver Committee were samples. Thousands of Chicago girls still try to look like Jean Harlow, although
they may never have heard of her. They style themselves on their older sisters, who picked up the idea
from their youngish mothers. All the men you see in
bars along streets like Rush and Division are in uni-

form as hoods. The hair shines, the hats are down over the eyes, the well-spaced-out orders for beer escape from the corners of the mouths, and with no need to punch the time clock in Goldblatt's department store until eight o'clock next morning, the boys are at liberty to listen to the two-piano team and look sinister. They also look terrified, because most of them believe that the other fellows in the bar, who probably work in Marshall Field's, may be what they are disguised as. The bar customers are loath to enter into conversation with strangers, lest they betray their own harmlessness and so become victims. Faith in the omnipresence of crime is like a belief in voodoo. It makes the believer cautious. I have witnessed a similiar aloofness at gatherings of unacquainted Englishmen, each afraid to betray by his accent that he has gone to a less important school than the others. Britons so situated open their mouths as hesitantly as poker players turn up their hole cards. The pleased smile of the fellow who finally takes the pot—perhaps an old boy of a small public school—is a lovely thing to watch. Now all he has to think of is something to say.

Chicago's working gangsters have gone mysterious.

They are referred to as the Syndicate, and it is accepted as gospel by congenial people that the Syndicate owns most of the good restaurants in the city, one
or two of the race tracks, and the laundry, dry-clean-
ing, candy, soda-water, baby-linen, night-club, antique-
glass, and beauty-parlor businesses, as well as the
labor unions, the public utilities, and any hotel a
visitor happens to be stopping at. "Did you know that
was a Syndicate place?" is a staple of small talk. The
answer is "Sure. Who doesn't know that?" The out-of-
towner's accompanying mental reservation is "Who
does?," but he should not voice it if he wishes to be
popular.

A while ago, the *Sun-Times*, in a series that purported to expose the Syndicate-operated call-girl system, yielded so unreservedly to Chicago's honest adu-
lation of its gangsters that the installments could have
been reprinted as a brochure for distribution by the
Chicago Convention Bureau. The girls, the *Sun-Times*
reported, were beautiful and well dressed, and, thanks
to efficient Syndicate administration of the system, the
out-of-town customer was reasonably free from worry
about blackmail, larceny, or venereal disease. All of

these were discouraged, the *Sun-Times* recorded, because of their effect on customer good will. To meet a girl, the reader was advised, the visitor applied to the bell captain in his hotel. The day after the first article appeared, Milburn P. Akers, who was then the *Sun-Times'* managing editor, got a letter from a girl who said she was a waitress and would like to know how to get a job as a call girl.

Syndicate administration of the saloon-with-entertainment business is equally smooth, a man on a theatrical publication told me. "In the twenties, two or three different outfits might try to muscle in on the same place," he said. "If the fellow didn't pay off, they went in for rough stuff, and even if he did, they might get rough with each other. Now just one man arrives and says he is from City Hall, and he is a partner, drawing down a hundred and a half a week, or two hundred—whatever the club looks good for. It's a part of the nut, like the rent. After all, if everybody has to pay, nobody has an unfair advantage."

"And if the place doesn't pay off?" I asked.

"The police send a delinquent female minor into the joint to buy a drink," my informant replied.

"Some kid who looks over eighteen and will do anything they say because she's out on parole. The law is death on selling drinks to minors. Then they close the place."

"But is the fellow who declares himself in really from City Hall or from the Syndicate?" I asked.

"Well, he's known as a Syndicate fellow, but the police enforce what he says," the man said. "I don't know what the split is."

"Maybe the Syndicate is just a front for the city government," I suggested, "instead of its being the other way around." [3]

....

[3] The story of Sammy Rinella, murdered last December, several months after the above was written, seems to lend some support to this hypothesis. Rinella, a night-club promoter, had not included in his 1945 income-tax return a bank deposit of $157,000. When the Internal Revenue people, reviewing his return, challenged this omission in 1951, Rinella said the money hadn't been his. He said it had been part of $205,000 he had borrowed from a police captain so he could open a new night club. Rinella was shot to death soon after he told his story. The police captain admitted having lent him some money—a mere $100,000. But he denied any connection with the shooting.

In the old days the boys staked the cops. Now, it appears, the cops stake the boys.

142

And maybe, I have thought since, the city government is just a front for Colonel McCormick and for the railroads that don't want to be moved off the streets and for the landlords who don't want to lose the swollen rents from their hovels and for all the nice, earnest people who constantly form committees but really don't want anything changed if it costs money. If no Syndicate existed, it would be necessary to invent one, to blame it for the way things are. The leaders of the Syndicate, whoever they may be, hardly ever shoot each other in public any more, even one at a time, and Chicagoans are left in the plight of the Greeks at the beginning of history, when the gods commenced ceasing to manifest themselves.

Newspapers made much of the fact the police captain, who is now retired, never made more than $5,200 a year. The implication was that he must have been a paragon of thrift. But suppose the $100,000 or $205,000 had been his only in part, or not at all. Might he not have been acting for a departmental investment fund, a kind of police-force Morris Plan?

A NOTE ON THE TYPE

....

This book was composed on the Linotype in BODONI BOOK, so called after Giambattista Bodoni (1740–1813), son of a printer of Piedmont. After gaining experience and fame as superintendent of the Press of the Propaganda in Rome, Bodoni became in 1768 the head of the ducal printing house at Parma, which he soon made the foremost of its kind in Europe. His Manuale Tipografico, completed by his widow in 1818, contains 279 pages of specimens of types, including alphabets of about thirty languages. His editions of Greek, Latin, Italian, and French classics are celebrated for their typography. In type-designing he was an innovator, making his new faces rounder, wider, and lighter, with greater openness and delicacy.

Composed, printed, and bound by H. WOLFF, New York. Designed by HARRY FORD; photo-drawing for binding by STEINBERG.

DATE DUE